40-Day Journey with Julian of Norwich

Other books in the

40-DAY *Journey* Series

40-Day Journey with Joan Chittister
Beverly Lanzetta, Editor

40-Day Journey with Dietrich Bonhoeffer
Ron Klug, Editor

40-Day Journey with Martin Luther
Gracia M. Grindal, Editor

40-Day Journey with Kathleen Norris
Kathryn Haueisen, Editor

40-Day Journey with Parker J. Palmer
Harry F. French, Editor

40-DAY
Journey

WITH JULIAN OF NORWICH

40-Day Journey Series

Lisa E. Dahill, Editor

Augsburg Books
Minneapolis

Cover art: Photo © Bildarchive Preussisches Kultusbasitz/Art Resource, NY
Cover design: Christy Barker
Interior design and composition: PerfecType, Nashville, Tenn.

Library of Congress Cataloging-in-Publication Data
Dahill, Lisa E.
40-day journey with Julian of Norwich / Lisa E. Dahill, editor.
    p. cm. — (40-day journey series)
Includes bibliographical references.
ISBN 978-0-8066-8047-7 (alk. paper)
1. Julian, of Norwich, b. 1343. 2. Devotional literature. 3. Mysticism. I. Title.

BV5095.J84D34 2008
242--dc22
        2008022189

CONTENTS

SERIES INTRODUCTION

Imagine spending forty days with a great spiritual guide who has both the wisdom and the experience to help you along the path of your own spiritual journey. Imagine being able to listen to and question spiritual guides from the past and the present. Imagine being, as it were, mentored by women and men who have made their own spiritual journey and have recorded the landmarks, detours, bumps in the road, potholes, and wayside rests that they encountered along the way—all to help others (like you) who must make their own journey.

The various volumes in Augsburg Books' *40-Day Journey Series* are all designed to do just that—to lead you where your mind and heart and spirit long to go. As Augustine once wrote: *"You have made us for yourself, O Lord, and our heart is restless until it rests in you."* The wisdom you will find in the pages of this series of books will give you the spiritual tools and direction to find that rest. But there is nothing quietistic in the spirituality you will find here. Those who would guide you on this journey have learned that the heart that rests in God is one that lives with deeper awareness, deeper creativity, deeper energy, and deeper passion and commitment to the things that matter to God.

An ancient Chinese proverb states the obvious: the journey of a thousand miles begins with the first step. In a deep sense, books in the *40-Day Journey Series* are first steps on a journey that will not end when the forty days are over. No one can take the first step (or any step) for you.

Imagine that you are on the banks of the Colorado River. You are here to go white-water rafting for the first time and your guide has just described the experience, telling you with graphic detail what to expect. It sounds both exciting and frightening. You long for the experience but are somewhat disturbed, anxious, uncertain in the face of the danger that promises to accompany you on the journey down the river. The guide gets into the raft. She will accompany you on the journey, *but she can't take the journey for you.* If you want to experience the wildness of the river, the raw beauty of the canyon, the camaraderie of adventurers, and the mystery of a certain oneness with nature (and nature's creator), then you've got to get in the boat.

This book in your hand is like that. It describes the journey, provides a "raft," and invites you to get in. Along with readings from your spiritual guide, you will find scripture to mediate on, questions to ponder, suggestions for personal journaling, guidance in prayer, and a prayer for the day. If done faithfully each day, you will find the wisdom and encouragement you need to integrate meaningful spiritual insights and practices into your daily life. And when the 40-day journey is over it no longer will be the guide's description of the journey that stirs your longing for God but *your own experience* of the journey that grounds your faith and life and keeps you on the path.

I would encourage you to pick up other books in the series. There is only one destination, but many ways to get there. Not everything in every book will work for you (we are all unique), but in every book you will find much to help you discover your own path on the journey to the One in whom we all "live and move and have our being" (Acts 17:28).

May all be well with you on the journey
Henry F. French, Series Editor

PREFACE

Know it well, love was his meaning. Who reveals it to you? Love. What did he reveal to you? Love. Why does he reveal it to you? For love. Remain in this, and you will know more of the same. But you will never know different, without end.[1]

This book is an invitation to spend time in the company of one of the greatest Christian mystics of all time: Julian of Norwich. Living in fourteenth-century England, Julian knew firsthand the traumas of war, plague, and social upheaval. Yet her writings testify to visions of Jesus Christ bringing her—and all those who read her work—a message of extraordinary love and hope.

Journeying forty days with Julian will invite you deep into her encounter with the One who loves you (and all things) passionately, intimately, and securely. It will also open you to a theologian whose lifelong probing of her experience of God has provided insight rarely matched in any generation. Rowan Williams, Archbishop of Canterbury and an influential historian and theologian, considers her *Showings* "what may well be the most important work of Christian reflection in the English language."[2]

Showings is a work that:

- Takes seriously biblical truth and doctrinal heritage, yet with the freedom to experience God in ways the church hasn't yet explored.
- Opens the encompassing, radical nature of God's grace and mercy in ways that prefigure the Reformation a century later, while remaining fully rooted in the piety of its own time.
- Invites readers into an encounter with Jesus experienced as Mother, within a profoundly Trinitarian spirituality and a deeply relational openness to all people, indeed, to all the cosmos.

- Takes seriously the reality of sin and evil in the world and invites the perception of God endlessly, patiently, joyfully at work redeeming people and all things in their brokenness.
- Is saturated on every page with hope, delight, and the love and mercy of God, glimpsed in deep trust by a soul devoted to Jesus Christ.

Reading any medieval writer presents a glimpse into a world different in many ways from our own. Here (as with Martin Luther's writings) God and the devil are often understood and experienced as addressing human beings directly. Here the insights and visions received from God are taken seriously as sources of truth. And this truth takes shape in symbolic form, as the encounter with God unfolds through the images of a crucifix, a hazelnut, and the relationships between lord and servant or mother and child. As when we work with our dreams, here too we are invited to encounter the symbols and images directly, on their own terms, and let God touch us in them.

This encounter with Julian will draw you deep into the mystery of God's unending love for you, while giving you all the space you need to respond with authentic freedom. I look forward to journeying these days with you!

In our creation we had beginning,
but the love in which he created us was in him from without beginning.
In this love we have our beginning, and all this shall we see in God without end. [3]

—Lisa E. Dahill

HOW TO USE THIS BOOK

Your 40-day journey with Julian of Norwich gives you the opportunity to be mentored by a great contemporary spiritual writer and Christian leader. The purpose of the journey, however, is not just to gain "head knowledge" about Julian of Norwich. Rather, it is to begin living what you learn.

You will probably benefit most by fixing a special time of day in which to "meet with" your spiritual mentor. It is easier to maintain a spiritual practice if you do it regularly at the same time. For many people, mornings, while the house is still quiet and before the busyness of the day begins, is a good time. Others will find that the noon hour or before bedtime serves well. We are all unique. Some of us are "morning people" and some of us are not. Do whatever works *for you* to maintain a regular meeting with Julian of Norwich. Write it into your calendar and do your best to keep your appointments.

It is best if you complete your 40-day journey in forty days. A deepening focus and intensity of experience will be the result. However, it is certainly better to complete the journey than to give it up because you can't get it done in forty days. Indeed, making it a 40- or 20-week journey may better fit your schedule and it just might be that spending a whole week, or perhaps half a week, reflecting on the reading, the scripture, and the prayers, and then practicing what you are learning, could be a powerfully transforming experience as well. Again, set a schedule that works for you, only be consistent.

Each day of the journey begins with a reading from Julian of Norwich. You will note that the readings, from day to day, build on each other and introduce you to key ideas in her understanding of Christian life and faith. Read each selection slowly, letting the words sink into your consciousness. You may want to read each selection two or three times before moving on, perhaps reading it out loud once.

Following the reading from Julian of Norwich's writings, you will find the heading *Biblical Wisdom* and a brief passage from the Bible that relates directly to what she has said. As with the selection from Julian, read the biblical text slowly, letting the words sink into your consciousness.

Following the biblical reading, you will find the heading *Silence for Meditation*. Here you should take anywhere from five to twenty minutes meditating on the two readings. Begin by getting centered. Sit with your back straight, eyes closed, hands folded in your lap, and breathe slowly and deeply. Remember that breath is a gift of God, it is God's gift of life. Do nothing for two or three minutes other than simply observe your breath. Focus your awareness on the end of your nose. Feel the breath enter through your nostrils and leave through your nostrils.

Once you feel your mind and spirit settling down, open your eyes and read both the daily reading and the biblical text again. Read them slowly, focus on each word or phrase, savor them, explore possible meanings and implications. At the end of each day you will find a blank space with the heading *Notes*. As you meditate on the readings, jot down any insights that occur to you. Do the readings raise any questions for you? Write them down. Do the readings suggest anything you should do? Write it down.

Stay at it as long as it feels useful. When your mind is ready to move on, close your eyes and observe your breath for a minute or so. Then return to the book and the next heading: *Questions to Ponder*. Here you will find a few pointed questions by Lisa Dahill, the book's compiler and editor, on the day's reading. These are general questions intended for all spiritual seekers and communities of faith. Think them through and write your answers (and the implications of your answers for your own life of faith and for your community of faith) in the *Notes* section.

Many of these *Questions to Ponder* are designed to remind us—as Julian of Norwich would affirm—that although spirituality is always personal, it is simultaneously relational and communal. A number of the questions, therefore, apply the relevance of the day's reading to faith communities. Just remember, a faith community may be as large as a regular organized gathering of any religious tradition, or as small as a family, or the relationship between spiritual friends. You don't need to be a member of a church, synagogue, mosque, or temple to be part of a faith community. Answer the questions in the context of your particular faith community.

Then move on to the heading *Psalm Fragment*. Here you will find a brief verse or two from the Hebrew book of Psalms that relate to the day's reading. The Psalms have always been the mainstay of prayer in the Christian tradition and always speak to the real situations in which we find ourselves—the kind of realism with which Julian of Norwich's teaching and life resonate.

Reflect for a moment on the *Psalm Fragment* and then continue on to the heading *Journal Reflections*. Several suggestions for journaling are given that apply the readings to your own personal experience. It is in journaling that the "day" reaches its climax and the potential for transformative change is greatest. It would be best to buy a separate journal rather than use the *Notes* section of the book. For a journal you can use a spiral-bound or ring-bound notebook or one of the hardcover journal books sold in stationery stores. Below are some suggestions for how to keep a journal. For now, let's go back to the 40-day journey book.

The *Questions to Ponder* and *Journal Reflections* exercises are meant to assist you in reflecting on the daily reading and scripture quotations. Do not feel that you have to answer every question. You may choose which questions or exercises are most helpful to you. Sometimes a perfectly appropriate response to a question is "I don't know" or "I'm not sure what I think about that." The important thing is to record your own thoughts and questions.

After *Journal Reflections*, you will find two more headings. The first is *Prayers of Hope & Healing*. One of the highest services a person of faith can perform is prayer for family and friends, for one's community of faith, for the victims of injustice, and for one's enemies. Under this heading you will find suggestions for prayer that relate to the key points in the day's readings. The last heading (before *Notes*) is *Prayer for Today*, a one- or two-line prayer to end your "appointment" with Julian of Norwich, and to be prayed from time to time throughout the day.

Hints on Keeping a Journal

A journal is a very helpful tool. Keeping a journal is a form of meditation, a profound way of getting to know yourself—and God—more deeply. Although you could read your 40-day journey book and reflect on it "in your head," writing can help you focus your thoughts, clarify your thinking, and keep a record of your insights, questions, and prayers. Writing is generative: it enables you to have thoughts you would not otherwise have had.

A few hints for journaling

1. Write in your journal with grace. Don't get stuck in trying to do it perfectly. Just write freely. Don't worry about literary style, spelling, or grammar. Your goal is simply to generate thoughts pertinent to your own life and get them down on paper.
2. You may want to begin and end your journaling with prayer. Ask for the guidance and wisdom of the Spirit (and thank God for that guidance and wisdom when you are done).
3. If your journaling takes you in directions that go beyond the journaling questions in your 40-day book, go there. Let the questions encourage, not limit, your writing.
4. Respond honestly. Don't write what you think you're supposed to believe. Write down what you really do believe, in so far as you can identify that. If you don't know, or are not sure, or if you have questions, record those. Questions are often openings to spiritual growth.
5. Carry your 40-day book and journal around with you every day during your journey (only keep them safe from prying eyes). The 40-day journey process is an intense experience that doesn't stop when you close the book. Your mind and heart and spirit will be engaged all day, and it will be helpful to have your book and journal handy to take notes or make new entries as they occur to you.

Journeying with Others

You can use your 40-day book with another person—a spiritual friend or partner—or with a small group. It would be best for each person to first do his or her own reading, reflection, and writing in solitude. Then when you come together, share the insights you have gained from your time alone. Your discussion will probably focus on the *Questions to Ponder,* however, if the relationship is intimate, you may feel comfortable sharing some of what you have written in your journal. No one, however, should ever be pressured to share anything in their journal if they are not comfortable doing so.

Remember that your goal is to learn from one another, not to argue, nor to prove that you are right and the other person wrong. Just practice listening and trying to understand why your partner, friend, or colleague thinks as he or she does.

Practicing intercessory prayer together, you will find, will strengthen the spiritual bonds of those who take the journey together. And as you all work to translate insight into action, sharing your experience with each other is a way of encouraging and guiding each other and provides the opportunity to provide feedback to each other gently if that becomes necessary.

Continuing the Journey

When the forty days (or forty weeks) are over, a milestone has been reached, but the journey needn't end. One goal of the 40-day series is to introduce you to a particular spiritual guide with the hope that, having whet your appetite, you will want to keep the journey going. At the end of the book are some suggestions for further reading that will take you deeper on your journey with your mentor.

WHO WAS JULIAN OF NORWICH?

The mystic we know as Julian was born in 1342 or 1343, in or near Norwich in the northeastern portion of England. Norwich at the time was England's second-largest city, and it boasted a rich religious, artistic, and university life. Biographical data of Julian's life are scarce, but we know from her own writing that she was 30½ years old in May of 1373, when she had the visions of Jesus Christ that shaped the rest of her life and inspired the writing of her *Showings*. At that point she was mortally ill, weak, and racked with pain; she and those gathered thought she was on the brink of death.

The priest had given her last rites, and her mother was prepared to close Julian's eyes in death. But as she gazed at the crucifix placed before her she began instead to perceive what she later distinguished as sixteen "showings" of Christ, beginning with him on the cross as he too was dying. Her vision of Jesus' movement into death was graphic, yet its effect was to console her deeply. In seeing his blood, pain, and thirst on the cross, she heard Jesus reassuring her and perceived precisely there the love animating his entire life. Just as in the *St. Matthew Passion* J. S. Bach composed some of the most exquisitely beautiful music ever written to express the depth of love Jesus' crucifixion opened, so too for Julian the passion of Christ is pure gift, meeting us (like Julian) right where we are and bringing us into the very heart and bliss of God's victory over death.

Her visions continued throughout that day and the next. Two key promises the Lord gave her, woven in various forms throughout her writings, summarize the heart of the gift: "See how I love you!" and "All will be well." These rock-solid promises of divine love and hope transformed not only Julian's own life but also her understanding of God, human life, and reality itself. And this was no Pollyanna optimism; fourteenth-century England was a time of great upheaval. Nearly nonstop war between France and England had resulted in political instability and rebellions, and bubonic plague struck

Norwich three times during Julian's lifetime, resulting in widespread loss of life. Her spirituality of hope and grace speaks a new Word of life into a time of fear and uncertainty—and has the power to recast our own time of fear and uncertainty as well.

Julian recovered from her illness and ended up living at least forty more years. She spent the rest of her life pondering these extraordinary revelations. Soon after the visions she wrote what we now know as the "Short Text," a rather straightforward account of what she had experienced. But as she continued to reflect over the next twenty years and beyond, she began to plumb the depths and theological implications of Jesus' powerful revelation of love at the heart of Christian life. Ultimately she wrote what we know as the "Long Text" of her visions. In the Long Text, most of the Short Text is carefully preserved, retaining that work's immediacy and grounding in actual experience. But in addition, she weaves in, through, and around the Short Text the insight and further revelation that deepens into a work of incredible theological power. Several key portions of her legacy—the Mother-Jesus material and the Lord and Servant parable among them—are found only in the Long Text.

We don't know much more about Julian; her legacy to us is her actual writing, through which we glimpse her fine mind, prayerful heart, and love for God and her fellow Christians. We don't know her state of life at the time of her visions: Was she a nun? A wife and mother? We do know that at some point in her life, presumably following her visions, she was granted permission to become an *anchorite:* a monk or nun who lives a life of detachment from the world, living in a small cell (called an "anchorage") attached to a church, and vowing never to leave this cell for the rest of one's life. This way of life is modeled on the earliest Christian ascetics, who lived in the desert alone with God; in medieval times the anchorite remained in the community, in the public gaze though hidden from direct view. Upon taking the anchoritic vows, the monk or nun was sealed into the anchorage and had the Order of the Dead performed on his or her behalf, since from this point on she or he was considered dead to the world. In fact, we don't even know Julian's real name: "Julian" was the saint for whom the church to which she was attached was named, and upon her entrance to the anchorage she was known henceforth only by this borrowed name.

Despite their ritual seclusion, anchorites remained present as spiritual resources to the community, themselves dependent on the community and offering their gifts of spiritual direction, prayer, and teaching to others. The anchoritic way was considered a high and holy calling, modeling for the whole community the grace of a life devoted completely to God.

Julian's anchorage was probably just a few feet square, with two or possibly three windows. One window opened directly into the church, from which she could see the altar of the reserved sacrament, hear mass being conducted, and receive the sacrament; a second opened to the world and allowed Julian to receive food, water, and occasional contact from persons desiring counsel. Many anchorages also had a third window for light. Here in her cell, present to the worship of God and the needs of the world, Julian prayed and wrote her Long Text; she died sometime after 1416. Her writings are the earliest work we know to be written by a woman in English.

Julian's writing was largely unknown before surfacing in the seventeenth century, and she became widely known only in the twentieth century.[4] But despite her anonymity, Julian has left us a rich legacy: a treasure of Christian spirituality for the church of all times.

40-DAY

Journey

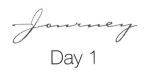

Day 1

GOD DOES NOT DESPISE WHAT he has made. . . . For as the body is clad
in the cloth, and the flesh in the skin, and the bones in the flesh, and
the heart in the trunk, so are we, soul and body, clad and enclosed in the
goodness of God. Yes, and more closely, for all these vanish and waste
away; the goodness of God is always complete, and closer to us, beyond
any comparison. For truly our lover desires the soul to adhere to him
with all its power, and us always to adhere to his goodness. . . . For it is
so preciously loved by him who is highest that this surpasses the knowledge of all created beings. That is to say, there is no created being who
can know how much and how sweetly and how tenderly the Creator
loves us. . . . God wishes to be seen, and he wishes to be sought, and he
wishes to be expected, and he wishes to be trusted.

~

BIBLICAL WISDOM

*In Christ Jesus you are all children of God through faith. As many of you as were
baptized into Christ have clothed yourselves with Christ.* Galatians 3:26-27

SILENCE FOR MEDITATION

QUESTIONS TO PONDER

- Julian says that God does not despise any creature, anything God has
  made. How does our having been lovingly created and formed and knit
  together by God affect how you see others? The earth? Your own body and
  soul and heart?
- How does Julian's imagery of being "clad and enclosed in the goodness of
  God" deepen your understanding of St. Paul's language of being "clothed
  . . . with Christ" through baptism?
- Julian states that God desires to be seen, sought, expected, and trusted.
  How might a faith community assist in the realization of God's desire?

PSALM FRAGMENT

*For it was you who formed my inward parts;
    you knit me together in my mother's womb.
I praise you, for I am fearfully and wonderfully made.
    Wonderful are your works;
that I know very well.* Psalm 139:13-14

JOURNALING REFLECTIONS

- God "does not despise what he has made." This includes you—always, with no exceptions! In fact, you are "preciously loved by [God]." Journal about how this makes you feel and rest in this love throughout the day.
- Julian says we are "soul and body, clad and enclosed in the goodness of God." Imagine yourself to be entirely wrapped in the reality of God's surpassing love, warmth, and goodness. What do you feel? Why?
- Describe in your journal aspects of your life, including any spiritual practices you follow, that open you to seeing, seeking, expecting, and trusting God. Are there practices you think would help you grow in this seeing, seeking, expecting, and trusting?

PRAYERS OF HOPE & HEALING

Pray for all who have suffered shame, abuse, or neglect that leads them to despise themselves. May they experience this God in whom there is mercy, healing, and complete acceptance.

PRAYER FOR TODAY

God of love, wrap me in your love today and hold me always close with that divine mercy in which my body was formed and knit together in your image. Give me grace to live this day seeing, seeking, expecting, and trusting you, through Jesus Christ our Lord. Amen.

NOTES

Seeing – God's bounty & human need
Seeking – ways of connecting God's bounty
    and our need
Expecting – God to act & to change me
Trusting – God's wisdom, goodness,
    providence, warmth, & love

Day 2

[AT THE POINT OF DEATH, Julian is gazing at a crucifix.] And at this, suddenly I saw the red blood running down from under the crown, hot and flowing freely and copiously, a living stream, just as it was at the time when the crown of thorns was pressed on his blessed head. I perceived, truly and powerfully, that it was he who just so, both God and man, himself suffered for me, who showed it to me without intermediary. And . . . suddenly the Trinity filled my heart full of the greatest joy, and I understood that it will be so in heaven without end to all who will come there. For the Trinity is God, God is the Trinity. The Trinity is our maker, the Trinity is our protector, the Trinity is our everlasting lover, the Trinity is our endless joy and our bliss, by our Lord Jesus Christ and in our Lord Jesus Christ. And this was revealed in the first vision and in them all, for where Jesus appears the blessed Trinity is understood. . . . The most important point to apprehend in his Passion is to meditate and come to see that he who suffered is God.

~

BIBLICAL WISDOM

He was wounded for our transgressions,
crushed for our iniquities; . . .
and by his bruises we are healed. Isaiah 53:5

SILENCE FOR MEDITATION

QUESTIONS TO PONDER

- What images of Jesus' crucifixion—scriptural, poetic, musical, or artistic—are most familiar to you? Do these images readily speak to you of love, as they do to Julian? Why or why not?
- For Julian, Jesus' death is not an appeasement of God's wrath. Rather, "the most important point to apprehend in [Jesus'] Passion is . . . that he who suffered *is* God." (Italics added.) What difference does it make for you to see Jesus not suffering under God's wrath but as *God* suffering?
- For Julian, to glimpse the face of Jesus is to be given the entire fullness of God,

for "where Jesus appears the blessed Trinity is understood." How does this statement correspond to how you or your faith community understands Jesus?

Psalm Fragment

I thank you that you have answered me
and have become my salvation.
The stone that the builders rejected
has become the chief cornerstone.
This is the LORD's doing;
it is marvelous in our eyes. Psalm 118:21-23

Journaling Reflections

- Julian is brought into the fullness of divine intimacy and personal presence through her meditation on the crucifix. Write about where you experience God's presence.
- The image of someone bleeding may stir disturbing memories for you of trauma or violence. Be careful if this image evokes raw wounds. Or it may stir deep compassion, grief, guilt, or some other feeling or reaction. Tell Jesus directly what feelings the image of the crucifixion stirs in you. Be as honest as you can: he is ready, as God, to receive in profound love whatever you might say, even if it shocks or surprises you. Listen for his response to your feelings. Journal your experience.
- For Julian, "the Trinity is our maker, the Trinity is our protector, the Trinity is our everlasting lover, the Trinity is our endless joy and our bliss." Which of these attributes of the Trinity is closest to your own image of God? Explain. Does Julian name new dimensions of God you would like to explore? If so, what are they?

Prayers of Hope & Healing

Pray for those who have had Jesus' suffering used to legitimate their own suffering. May the Crucified One release them from their pain and draw them with him into resurrection.

Prayer for Today

O triune God, our maker, protector, everlasting lover, our endless joy and bliss, I entrust myself and all the world to you today. Amen.

Notes

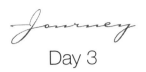

Day 3

AND IN THIS HE SHOWED me something small, no bigger than a hazelnut, lying in the palm of my hand, and I perceived that it was as round as any ball. I looked at it and thought: What can this be? And I was given this general answer: it is everything which is made. I was amazed that it could last, for I thought that it was so little that it could suddenly fall into nothing. And I was answered in my understanding: it lasts and always will, because God loves it; and thus everything has being through the love of God. . . . In this little thing I saw three properties. The first is that God made it, the second is that he loves it, and the third is that God preserves it.

BIBLICAL WISDOM

In the beginning, when God created the heavens and the earth . . . God saw everything that he had made, and indeed, it was very good. Genesis 1:1, 31a

SILENCE FOR MEDITATION

QUESTIONS TO PONDER

- Scientists tell us that the cosmos—"everything which is made"—is far beyond our minds' capacity to comprehend. Yet in Julian's vision, all of creation can be seen in something as small as a hazelnut in her palm. What of the Creator does this image open for you?
- Have you ever seen a photo of Earth from space? Imagine it like the hazelnut in Julian's vision, treasured and priceless to God. How does the vision of our Earth as infinitely treasured by God shape the way you treat creation in your everyday life and decisions?
- How might your faith community nurture a sense of the sacredness of the Earth to God?

PSALM FRAGMENT

When I look at your heavens, the work of your fingers,
the moon and the stars that you have established;
what are human beings that you are mindful of them,
mortals that you care for them? Psalm 8:3-4

JOURNAL REFLECTIONS

- The psalmist gazing at the expanse of stars is astonished at the mystery of God's regard for us within the endlessness of the cosmos. Write about experiences in your life that have caused a similar astonishment for you.
- Reread the final sentence in today's reading, substituting "me" for "it." What feelings or reactions does this prayer stir in you?
- Write how (if at all) time outdoors in creation helps to open you to the peace and awe of knowing yourself and all things sustained securely in God.

PRAYERS OF HOPE & HEALING

Pray for the earth and all its creatures, and for those who actively seek to embody God's sustaining love for the creation.

PRAYER FOR TODAY

Holy One, who calls the cosmos into being, give me eyes to see my life and all creation held securely in the palm of your hand. Amen.

NOTES

Journey

Day 4

IN THIS LITTLE THING [LIKE a hazelnut] I saw three properties. The first is that God made it, the second is that he loves it, and the third is that God preserves it. But what is that to me? It is that God is the Creator and the lover and the protector. For until I am substantially united to him, I can never have love or rest or true happiness; until, that is, I am so attached to him that there can be no created thing between my God and me. And who will do this deed? Truly, he himself, by his mercy and his grace, for he has made me for this and has blessedly restored me. . . . For this is the reason why those who deliberately occupy themselves with worldly business, constantly seeking worldly well-being, have not God's rest in their hearts and souls; for they love and seek their rest in this thing [that is, in all the cosmos, seemingly as small as a hazelnut] which is so little and in which there is no rest, and do not know God who is almighty, all wise and all good, for he is true rest.

BIBLICAL WISDOM

Strive first for the kingdom of God and his righteousness, and all these things will be given to you as well. Matthew 6:33

SILENCE FOR MEDITATION

QUESTIONS TO PONDER

- What do you think is the sort of "worldly business" Julian says cuts people off from God's rest?
- In your faith tradition, what is the appropriate balance between a "this-worldly" investment in human life and one's total commitment and allegiance to God? Can both be lived simultaneously? Explain.
- Becoming "substantially united to [God]" is impossible for us: "Who will do this . . . ?" Julian answers, "Truly, he himself, by his mercy and his grace" will do it for us. What does such grace mean for you?

Psalm Fragment

Behold the one who makes war to cease in all the world;
who breaks the bow,
and shatters the spear,
and burns the shields with fire.
"Be still, then, and know that I am God!" Psalm 46:9-10 (ELW)

Journal Reflections

- Julian describes God as our "true rest," in distinction from the cares of busy lives in which there is no rest. Christian practices like centering prayer invite people to learn to be still in God's love. Write about what helps you experience God as your "true rest."
- Each of us also has some compulsion or unmet need that can cut us off from rest and intimacy with God. In themselves these are not evil but are the places in us most in need of God. Write about what in your life needs to be opened to the healing, restorative love of God.
- Julian names as a goal of Christian life becoming united to God, such that "there can be no created thing between my God and me." Do you share this goal with Julian? If not, what is your own deepest desire for God? In either case, write about your desire.

Prayers of Hope & Healing

Pray for those who most need rest: parents of newborns, those working multiple jobs to survive, those juggling too many responsibilities, those who feel driven to push themselves or others too hard.

Prayer for Today

Lord Jesus, you invite all who are weary and heavy laden to come find their true rest in you. Help me hear your invitation spoken to me this day. Amen.

Notes

Day 5

IN THIS GOD BROUGHT OUR Lady [Jesus' mother, Mary] to my understanding. I saw her spiritually in her bodily likeness, a simple, humble maiden, young in years, of the stature which she had when she conceived. Also God showed me part of the wisdom and truth of her soul, and in this I understood the reverent contemplation with which she beheld her God, marveling with great reverence that he was willing to be born of her who was a simple creature created by him. And this wisdom and truth, this knowledge of her Creator's greatness and of her own created littleness, made her say meekly to the angel Gabriel: Behold me here, God's handmaiden.

⌁

BIBLICAL WISDOM

And Mary said, "My soul magnifies the Lord, and my spirit rejoices in God my Savior, for he has looked with favor on the lowliness of his servant."
Luke 1:46-48a

SILENCE FOR MEDITATION

QUESTIONS TO PONDER

- Is Julian's vision of Mary one you and your faith tradition would embrace? Why or why not? What is special for you about Mary?
- Julian appreciates the humility manifest in Mary's "reverence that [God] was willing to be born of her who was a simple creature created by him." How does our culture understand humility? How do you understand it? How does Julian's image recast understandings of humility that frame it as degrading?
- In what ways—and from what illusions—is true humility a liberating gift of God?

Psalm Fragment

To you, O Lord, I lift up my soul.
You lead the lowly in justice
and teach the lowly your way. Psalm 25: 1, 9 (ELW)

Journal Reflections

- Even in her "littleness" before God, Mary allowed great things to be done through her. In what ways, if any, do you experience yourself as "little"? How might God wish to stretch your perception of yourself or work through you at precisely those points?
- For both women and men throughout history, the image of Mary's pregnancy with God has proven fruitful in poetry, art, and meditation. Ponder what it might mean for you to be (metaphorically) "pregnant" with God. What might be growing toward birth in you?
- Mary's faith lies in her total availability to God, saying, in Julian's words, "Behold me here, God's handmaiden"—or, more simply: "Here I am!" What feelings does the prospect of total availability to God evoke in you? Can you pray, with Mary, "Here I am, Lord"? Why or why not?

Prayers of Hope & Healing

Pray for pregnant women and those in childbirth; those who struggle to conceive; adoptive and foster parents; all who give birth to God in the arts and other forms of creativity.

Prayer for Today

O God, right here in my littleness you desire to be born in me and through me. Give me trust and courage with Mary to open myself entirely to your love, your leading. Amen.

Notes

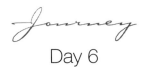

Day 6

IN [ALL] THIS DELIGHT I was filled full of everlasting surety, powerfully secured without any painful fear. This sensation was so welcome and so spiritual that I was wholly at peace, at ease and at rest, so that there was nothing upon earth which could have afflicted me. This lasted only for a time, and then I was changed, and abandoned to myself, oppressed and weary of my life and ruing myself, so that I hardly had the patience to go on living. . . . And then presently God gave me again comfort and rest for my soul. . . . And then again I felt the pain, and then afterwards the delight and joy, now the one and now the other, again and again, I suppose about twenty times. And in the time of joy I could have said with St. Paul: Nothing shall separate me from the love of Christ; and in the pain I could have said with St. Peter: Lord, save me, I am perishing. And so we remain in this mixture all the days of our life; but [what breaks the impasse is that Christ] wants us to trust that he is constantly with us.

⌐

BIBLICAL WISDOM

For I am convinced that neither death, nor life, nor angels, nor rulers, nor things present, nor things to come, nor powers, nor height, nor depth, nor anything else in all creation, will be able to separate us from the love of God in Christ Jesus our Lord. Romans 8:38-39

SILENCE FOR MEDITATION

QUESTIONS TO PONDER

- Julian reminds us that our faith is grounded on the presence of God in Jesus Christ rather than on fluctuations of mood that come and go. What is the danger of relying too heavily on one's present mood or feelings in gauging God's love for you?
- Julian notes that in her times of desolation she "hardly had the patience to go on living." For some who suffer depression, such feelings are distressingly familiar and can obscure the felt reality of God's love. What help might a faith community offer people in this situation?

- The book of Psalms is particularly important in learning to pray one's real, raw experience to God. Read through the book of Psalms. What psalms best express the pain, outrage, trust, or joy of your life?

PSALM FRAGMENT

In you, O LORD, I seek refuge. . . .
Incline your ear to me;
*   rescue me speedily.*
Be a rock of refuge for me,
*   a strong fortress to save me.* Psalm 31:1a, 2

JOURNAL REFLECTIONS

- Write about your times of highs and lows in prayer. What colors, symbols, or images might you use to draw them? What music gives voice to your experience?
- In referring to Paul and Peter, Julian invites us to let Scripture itself *pray our experience.* When you experience despair or need, are there any biblical stories or characters whose experience echoes yours? Does it help to find *your* experience in the Bible?
- With Luther, Julian reminds us that faith is what saves us: bare trustful clinging to Jesus who "wants us to trust that he is constantly with us." What helps to anchor your experience of God beyond your changing moods or shifting perceptions of yourself?

PRAYERS OF HOPE & HEALING

Pray for those in despair or depression; for those who cannot feel or sense God's presence; for the suicidal and for those who have lost loved ones to suicide.

PRAYER FOR TODAY

Lord Jesus, you descend into the depths of hell to free the souls there. Thank you for seeking me so faithfully in all my heights and depths. Amen.

NOTES

Day 7

OUR LORD WANTS TO HAVE the soul truly converted to contemplation of him and of all his works in general. For they are most good, and all his judgments are easy and sweet, bringing to great rest the soul which is converted from contemplating blind [human] judgments to the judgments, lovely and sweet, of our Lord God. . . . so long as we are in this life, whenever we in our folly revert to the contemplation of [others' misdeeds], our Lord tenderly teaches us and blessedly calls us, saying in our souls: . . . My beloved child, attend to me. I am enough for you, and rejoice in your savior and in your salvation. And I am sure that this is our Lord working in us. For the contemplation of other [people's] sins makes as it were a thick mist before the soul's eye, and during that time we cannot see the beauty of God, unless we can contemplate [these sins] with contrition with [the sinner], with compassion on [him or her], and with holy desires to God for [him or her].

BIBLICAL WISDOM

Do not judge, so that you may not be judged. Matthew 7:1

SILENCE FOR MEDITATION

QUESTIONS TO PONDER

- Julian notes that when we contemplate the sins of other people, it makes a thick mist before the soul's eye with the result that we cannot see the beauty of God. Does this ring true for you? Explain.
- How might one go about learning how not to judge themselves or others, but let God, whose judgments are "lovely and sweet," be judge? How might a community of faith help?
- Julian writes, "Our Lord wants to have the soul truly converted to contemplation of him." The Hebrew term for conversion means to turn from

a wrong way to a new direction. Reflect on experiences you have had of turning from the wrong direction in order to move toward God.

Psalm Fragment

To you I lift up my eyes,
  to you enthroned in the heavens.
As the eyes of servants
  look to the hand of their masters,
and the eyes of a maid
  to the hand of her mistress,
so our eyes look to you,
  O Lord our God,
  until you show us your mercy. Psalm 123:1-2 (ELW)

Journal Reflections

- Is it easy or difficult for you to experience Christ as judge as being "lovely and sweet" toward you rather than harsh? Write your response directly to him.
- What proportion of each day do you spend attending truly to God, contemplating God's endlessly loving regard for you and others, versus worrying about others' perceptions, judgments, and sins—or worrying about your own? Reflect on what pulls you away from attending to God.
- "My beloved child, attend to me. I am enough for you." Write these words of Jesus in your journal. Memorize them. Meditate on them all day.

Prayers of Hope & Healing

Pray for those who are often the target of others' judgment: the poor, the mentally ill, criminals, addicts. Pray for those parts of yourself you experience as impoverished, unstable, evil, or compulsive.

Prayer for Today

O Lord, you call me beloved and invite me to look away from my own faults and those of others to gaze on you alone. You are enough for me. Amen.

Notes

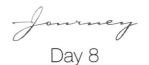

Day 8

[IN HER VISION OF JESUS' Passion, Julian writes:] "I saw in Christ a double thirst, one physical and the other spiritual. For insofar as Christ is our head, he is glorious and impassible; but with respect to his body to which all his members are joined, he is not fully glorified or wholly impassible. For he still has the same thirst and longing which he had upon the Cross, which desire, longing and thirst, as I see it, were in him from without beginning; and he will have this until the time that the last soul which will be saved has come up into his bliss. God's thirst is to have [us], generally, drawn into him, and in that thirst he has drawn his holy souls who are now in bliss. And so, gathering his living members, always he draws and drinks, and still he thirsts and he longs.

◡

BIBLICAL WISDOM

Those who drink of the water that I will give them will never be thirsty. The water that I will give will become in them a spring of water gushing up to eternal life. John 4:14

SILENCE FOR MEDITATION

QUESTIONS TO PONDER

- In her vision of Jesus' passion, Julian intensely experiences Jesus' thirst on the cross (John 19:28). What does it mean to say that the one who promises an endless spring of water to the Samaritan woman so that she will never be thirsty again is himself thirsty?
- Christ has a "double thirst, one physical and the other spiritual." We can understand his human thirst, but perhaps we don't often think of his divine heart thirsting. For what do you think God thirsts?
- In what ways does your faith community express the thirst of God?

Psalm Fragment

O God, you are my God, I seek you,
my soul thirsts for you;
my flesh faints for you,
as in a dry and weary land where there is no water. Psalm 63:1

Journal Reflections

- Deep thirst is an experience of almost unbearable physical intensity. Think of a time when you were truly thirsty. Does this metaphor describe your desire—or even longing—for God? Reflect in writing on the shape of your longing.
- Write about what helps to satisfy your thirst for God.
- The psalmist thirsts for the living God, and according to Julian, God thirsts for us too. What does it mean to you that God thirsts for you?

Prayers of Hope & Healing

Pray for all who suffer from unmanageable cravings, and for all those who do not have access to abundant, clean water to drink.

Prayer for Today

Lord Jesus, pour out your Spirit, the living water I thirst for. Let me drink from you as deeply as my heart desires. Amen.

Notes

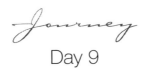

Day 9

AT THIS TIME I WANTED to look away from the cross, but I did not dare, for I knew well that whilst I contemplated the cross I was secure and safe. . . . Then there came a suggestion, seemingly said in a friendly manner, to my reason: Look up to heaven to his Father. . . . I answered inwardly with all the power of my soul, and said: No, I cannot, for you are my heaven. I said this because I did not want to look up, for I would rather have remained in that pain until Judgment Day than have come to heaven any other way than by him. . . . So was I taught to choose Jesus for my heaven, whom I saw only in pain at that time. No other heaven was pleasing to me than Jesus, who will be my bliss when I am there.

BIBLICAL WISDOM

When I came to you, brothers and sisters, I did not come proclaiming the mystery of God to you in lofty words or wisdom. For I decided to know nothing among you except Jesus Christ, and him crucified. 1 Corinthians 2:1-2

SILENCE FOR MEDITATION

QUESTIONS TO PONDER

- We might often prefer to have Jesus, or Christianity, or access to God, without the cross. Why does Julian reject this option? What does your faith community teach about the meaning of the crucifixion in giving us access to God?
- Christians sometimes interpret their suffering, or the suffering of others, as alienation from God, but Julian experiences her pain opening to the love and presence of Jesus crucified—that is, to God. Have you ever sensed God present in your or someone else's suffering? Explain.

- Julian is not writing about the validity of other religions' approaches to heaven or God, but this is an important question in our day. What does your faith community teach about non-Christian religions and their access to God? Do you agree with your faith community? Why or why not?

Psalm Fragment

Lord, you have been our dwelling place
  in all generations. . . .
  from everlasting to everlasting you are God. Psalm 90:1, 2c

Journal Reflections

- Write about what heaven is like in your prayerful imagination. Can you echo Julian's assertion that "Jesus [is] my heaven"—or does heaven have some other shape for you? Explain.
- Jesus blesses children, heals lepers, welcomes sinners, feeds the hungry, loves his tormenters, and so reveals the reality of heaven on earth. In what gospel story does Jesus reveal most fully the reality of heaven on earth for you? Write about this.
- For Julian, when gazing on the face of the Crucified One, she is "secure and safe." Write about what makes you feel secure and safe in times of crisis or despair.

Prayers of Hope & Healing

Pray for those who have no home in which to feel secure and safe: refugees, exiles, the homeless, those without love; and for all who are in chronic pain.

Prayer for Today

O God, you are my refuge and my secure dwelling place. Thank you for your presence in my places of suffering. Amen.

Notes

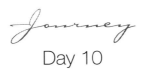

Day 10

"With this the fiend is overcome." Our Lord said this to me with reference to his blessed Passion, as he had shown it before. In this he showed a part of the fiend's malice, and all of his impotence, because he showed that his Passion is the overcoming of the fiend. . . . Also I saw our Lord scorn [the devil's] malice and despise him as nothing, and he wants us to do so. Because of this sight I laughed greatly, and that made those around me to laugh as well; and their laughter was pleasing to me . . . for I understood that we may laugh, to comfort ourselves and rejoice in God, because the devil is overcome.

Biblical Wisdom

Since, therefore, the children share flesh and blood, he himself likewise shared the same things, so that through death he might destroy the one who has the power of death, that is, the devil, and free those who all their lives were held in slavery by the fear of death. Hebrews 2:14-15

Silence for Meditation

Questions to Ponder

- Julian rejoices that Jesus' death destroys the power of the devil. Here God actually enters death, descends into hell, and gathers up those imprisoned there to bear them into resurrection. What reactions does this evoke in you?
- What does your faith community believe about the devil and hell? Do you agree? Why or why not?
- Do you believe with Julian that in Jesus' human flesh and blood *God* enters death to overcome it? In your faith, what is "good" about Good Friday?

PSALM FRAGMENT

The LORD is my light and my salvation;
  whom shall I fear?
The LORD is the stronghold of my life;
  of whom shall I be afraid?
When evildoers assail me
  to devour my flesh—
my adversaries and foes—
  they shall stumble and fall. Psalm 27:1-2

JOURNAL REFLECTIONS

- What "adversaries" or "foes" oppress your life and threaten your well-being? Write a prayer to Jesus telling him from what hell or captivity you long to be freed.
- Hear Jesus' words announcing clearly that the powers of sin and hell that bind *you* are overcome. What does that mean to you? In your daily life? In your hope for the world?
- Julian declares that Jesus wants us to scorn the devil's malice and despise him as nothing just as Jesus did. In what ways do you (or do you not) follow Jesus' bidding?

PRAYERS OF HOPE & HEALING

Pray for all who are living in hell and see no way out; for those in prison or in situations of domestic violence; for addicts; for the despairing. Pray for all who help us to laugh and trust.

PRAYER FOR TODAY

Lord Jesus, you break the power of hell and release those imprisoned. Free me from all that keeps me bound, that I may worship you with delight and joy. Amen.

NOTES

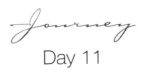
THEN OUR GOOD LORD PUT a question to me: Are you well satisfied that I suffered for you? I said: Yes, good Lord, all my thanks to you. . . . Then Jesus our good Lord said: If you are satisfied, I am satisfied. It is a joy, a bliss, an endless delight to me that ever I suffered my Passion for you; and if I could suffer more, I would suffer more. . . . For although the sweet humanity of Christ could suffer only once, his goodness can never cease offering it. . . . The love which made him suffer it surpasses all his sufferings, as much as heaven is above earth.

BIBLICAL WISDOM

Having loved his own who were in the world, he loved them to the end.
John 13:1b

SILENCE FOR MEDITATION

QUESTIONS TO PONDER

- Yesterday we explored how Jesus' death breaks the power of all that keeps us in bondage. In concrete, practical terms, how do you name what it means to say that Jesus suffered "for you"? From what captivity does his descent into hell release you?
- The Gospel of John sees *love* as the key to understanding Jesus' crucifixion: ". . . he loved [his own] to the end." Julian asserts that this love "surpasses all his sufferings." Do you see love in Jesus' death? If yes, in what ways? If not, why not?
- How does your faith community explain the death of Jesus? Does this explanation answer your questions? Explain.

Psalm Fragment

Bless the Lord, O my soul. . . .
who redeems your life from the Pit,
who crowns you with steadfast love and mercy,
who satisfies you with good as long as you live. Psalm 103:1a, 4-5a

Journal Reflections

- Have you ever experienced no-strings-attached sacrificial love from someone? If yes, write about the experience and its impact on you. If no, imagine what such an experience might be like for you.
- Have you ever experienced another person's claim to have sacrificed for you as an attempt to coerce or manipulate you? If so, write about the experience and its impact on you. In comparison, what feelings are evoked by Jesus' statement to Julian that "it is a joy, a bliss, an endless delight to me [to have suffered] for you"?
- Write your answer to the question Julian heard from Jesus in her vision: "Are you well satisfied that I suffered for you?"

Prayers of Hope & Healing

Pray for all who sacrifice themselves in love for others: parents for growing children, children for aging parents, caretakers of the sick, those who give sacrificially to help the poor, those whose gifts are never known or acknowledged.

Prayer for Today

O God, your love poured out in Jesus washes over each human being personally. Help me bathe in this love today and let it spill out to others through me. Amen.

Notes

AND WITH THE BEHOLDING OF [Jesus' Passion] . . . I did not see sin, for I believe that it has no kind of substance, no share in being, nor can it be recognized except by the pain caused by it. And it seems to me that this pain is something for a time, for it purges and makes us know ourselves and ask for mercy; for the Passion of our Lord is comfort to us against all this. . . . And because of the tender love which our good Lord has for all who will be saved, he comforts readily and sweetly, meaning this: It is true that sin is the cause of all this pain, but all will be well, and all will be well, and all manner of thing will be well. These words were revealed most tenderly, showing no kind of blame to me or to anyone who will be saved. So I saw how Christ has compassion on us because of sin.

BIBLICAL WISDOM

Come to me, all you that are weary and are carrying heavy burdens, and I will give you rest. Take my yoke upon you, and learn from me; for I am gentle and humble in heart, and you will find rest for your souls. For my yoke is easy, and my burden is light. Matthew 11:28-30

SILENCE FOR MEDITATION

QUESTIONS TO PONDER

- Julian teaches that sin can be recognized only by the pain it causes. Does this ring true to your experience? How do you tend to recognize sin in yourself or others?
- Sin, Julian believes, has "no kind of substance, no share in being." It is like a shadow, visible only by the darkness cast when love is obscured. How does this understanding compare to your faith community's teachings about sin?

- It might surprise us that Julian sees no divine anger for sin, but only mercy. Do you typically feel compassion for yourself when faced with your own sin? Explain. Do you have compassion for others in the face of their sin? Explain.

Psalm Fragment

Ours sins are stronger than we are,
  but you blot out our transgressions.
Happy are they whom you choose
  and draw to your courts, to dwell there!
They will be satisfied by the beauty of your house,
  by the holiness of your temple. Psalm 65:4-5 (ELW)

Journal Reflections

- From what are you presently weary? Are you carrying heavy burdens? Write about the effect of Jesus' words of rest and relief in Matthew 11 on you.
- In what ways has the pain of sin helped you to know yourself better?
- In her vision, Julian receives the assurance that, despite the pain of sin, "all will be well, and all will be well, and all manner of thing will be well." What feelings does this assurance evoke for you in your present situation?

Prayers of Hope & Healing

Pray for those who fear that their burden of sin is too heavy even for God, that they may experience the relief of mercy. Pray for all who are carrying heavy burdens of any kind.

Prayer for Today

O God, you are my strength when I'm weary, and you never cease to love me. Help me live this day belonging completely to you. Amen.

Notes

I STOOD, CONTEMPLATING [THESE THINGS] generally, darkly and mournfully, saying . . . to our Lord with very great fear: Ah, good Lord, how could all things be well, because of the great harm which has come through sin to your creatures? . . . And to this our blessed Lord answered, very meekly and with a most loving manner . . . that I should contemplate the glorious atonement, for this atoning is more pleasing to the blessed divinity and more honorable for [our] salvation, without comparison, than ever Adam's sin was harmful. [He said]: For since I have set right the greatest of harms, then it is my will that you should know through this that I shall set right everything which is less. . . . You will see yourself that every kind of thing will be well. [For] there are many deeds which in our eyes are so evilly done and lead to such great harms that it seems to us impossible that any good result could ever come of them. And we contemplate this and sorrow and mourn in it so that we cannot rest in the blessed contemplation of God as we ought to do.

~

BIBLICAL WISDOM

The thought of my affliction and my homelessness
  is wormwood and gall!
My soul continually thinks of it
  and is bowed down within me.
But this I call to mind,
  and therefore I have hope:
The steadfast love of the LORD never ceases,
  his mercies never come to an end;
they are new every morning;
  great is your faithfulness. Lamentations 3:19-23

SILENCE FOR MEDITATION

QUESTIONS TO PONDER

- Julian is contemplating "the great harm which has come through sin to [God's] creatures." What kinds of harm caused by sin disturb you most powerfully? Why do you think our culture avoids talking about sin?
- Julian asserts that contemplating sin and its effects can lead us to despair and cause us to forget about the reality of God who redeems all things. What helps you when you are tempted to despair?
- Is turning away from obsession with sin to contemplate God's redeeming love merely escapism, avoidance of the world's pain? In what ways might the contemplation of Christ lead us into the world in new ways?

PSALM FRAGMENT

But my eyes are turned toward you, O GOD, my Lord;
in you I seek refuge; do not leave me defenseless. Psalm 141:8

JOURNAL REFLECTIONS

- In Julian's vision, Jesus says, "I shall set right everything . . . every kind of thing will be well." Think of the realities of your own life, the lives of others, our society, the world, even the earth itself. Do you (or do you not) have trouble trusting that "all will be well"? Explain.
- Trying to suppress our fears only gives them more power. Write a prayer expressing your fears, then be still and listen for God's response.
- Julian reminds us that what our hearts and minds are fixed on shapes us, forms us, reveals where we put our trust. What is your heart and mind fixed on? How does it shape you? Write about what distracts your gaze from the love of God for yourself and our world.

PRAYERS OF HOPE & HEALING

Pray for all persons, animals, plants, ecosystems, and oceans ravaged by human sin, that "every kind of thing will be well."

PRAYER FOR TODAY

O God, you hold all our world's pain in your arms. Help me release to you all my fears for the future, trusting that you will indeed make all things well. Amen.

NOTES

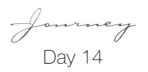

Day 14

BY SAYING, EVERY KIND OF thing will be well, . . . our good Lord
[Jesus] . . . wants us to know that he takes heed not only of things
which are noble and great, but also of those which are little and small,
of humble [people] and simple, of this [person] and that [one]. And this
is the supreme friendship of our courteous Lord, that he protects us so
tenderly whilst we are in our sins; and furthermore he touches us most
secretly, and shows us our sins by the sweet light of mercy and grace. But
when we see ourselves so foul, then we believe that God may be angry
with us. . . . Then we are moved by the Holy Spirit through contrition
to prayer, and we desire with all our might an amendment of ourselves.
. . . And then our courteous Lord shows himself to the soul, happily and
with the gladdest countenance, welcoming it as a friend, as if it had been
in pain and in prison, saying: My dear darling, I am glad that you have
come to me in all your woe. I have always been with you, and now you
see me loving, and we are made one in bliss.

BIBLICAL WISDOM

*[Jesus] said to Simon [the Pharisee], "Do you see this woman? I entered your
house; you gave me no water for my feet, but she has bathed my feet with her tears
and dried them with her hair. You gave me no kiss, but from the time I came in
she has not stopped kissing my feet. You did not anoint my head with oil, but she
has anointed my feet with ointment. Therefore, I tell you, her sins, which were
many, have been forgiven; hence she has shown great love. But the one to whom
little is forgiven, loves little." Luke 7:44-47*

SILENCE FOR MEDITATION

QUESTIONS TO PONDER

- For Julian, the glimpse of her sin leads not to despair but to prayerful,
  repentant love of the one who forgives and embraces her in joy. What part
  does contrition play in this process? What does your faith community
  teach about contrition as part of grace?

- Julian experiences God as one who cares for all people, including the little people, the humble, the simple, not just the great and noble. How, if at all, does this truth shape the mission and ministry of your faith community?
- Read Luke 7:36-50. Compare Jesus' and Simon's different responses to the woman. When you see evidence of others' sin, do you tend to respond like Jesus or Simon? What about when you are faced with your own sin?

PSALM FRAGMENT

Keep me as the apple of your eye;
  hide me under the shadow of your wings. Psalm 17:8 (ELW)

JOURNAL REFLECTIONS

- In your journal, if you have had such an experience, describe a time when you have come to Jesus "in all your woe." What was the result? If you haven't had such an experience, can you picture yourself doing it? Explain.
- Julian speaks of heartfelt friendship with Jesus. Do you experience Jesus as a friend? If so, in what ways? If not, how do you experience him?
- Julian and the woman in Luke 7 find that bringing their true selves to Jesus—sin and all—leads to intimacy, grace, and transformation, which would have been impossible if they had hidden themselves from him in shame. Have you ever felt completely loved for who you are?

PRAYERS OF HOPE & HEALING

Pray for those who are in pain and in prison, whether physically or spiritually (or both), and for those who struggle with being judgmental of others' sin and their own.

PRAYER FOR TODAY

Lord God, guard me as the apple of your eye; hide me in the shadow of your wings. Amen.

NOTES

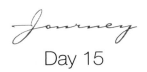

Day 15

[GOD] REGARDS SIN AS SORROW and pains for his lovers, to whom for love he assigns no blame. . . . For our courteous Lord does not want his servants to despair because they fall often and grievously; for our falling does not hinder him in loving us. No more than his love towards us is withdrawn because of our sin does he wish our love to be withdrawn from ourselves or from our fellow Christians. God also showed me that sin is no shame, but honor to [us], for in this vision my understanding was lifted up into heaven; and then there came truly to my mind David, Peter and Paul, Thomas of India, and Mary Magdalen, how they are known, with their sins, to their honor in the Church on earth. And it is to them no shame that they have sinned—shame is no more in the bliss of heaven—for there the tokens of sin are turned into honors. Just so our Lord showed them to me as examples of all who will come there.

BIBLICAL WISDOM

The saying is sure and worthy of full acceptance, that Christ Jesus came into the world to save sinners—of whom I am the foremost. But for that very reason I received mercy, so that in me, as the foremost, Jesus Christ might display the utmost patience, making me an example to those who would come to believe in him for eternal life. 1 Timothy 1:15-16

SILENCE FOR MEDITATION

QUESTIONS TO PONDER

- Julian points to the paradox of human sin and brokenness being places where God's love and mercy and power are all the more fully revealed. How have you experienced this paradox in your life or the lives of people you know?

- Does Julian's understanding of God as assigning no blame for sin lead to a "whitewashing" of sin? Why or why not?
- Julian declares that "shame is no more in the bliss of heaven." We live in a world where shaming is all too common. How might a faith community help in addressing and healing shame?

PSALM FRAGMENT

LORD, you are full of compassion and mercy,
slow to anger and abounding in steadfast love. . . .
You have not dealt with us according to our sins,
nor repaid us according to our iniquities.
For as the heavens are high above the earth,
so great is your steadfast love for those who fear you.
As far as the east is from the west,
so far have you removed our transgressions from us.
Psalm 103:8, 10-12 (ELW)

JOURNAL REFLECTIONS

- Julian declares that our falling (sin) does not hinder God in loving us. Is that easy or difficult for you to believe? Explain.
- What do you make of Julian's claim that God assigns no blame to us for our sin?
- Meditate on Julian's statement that God "does not want his servants to despair because they fall often and grievously." Journal about how this makes you feel. What are its implications for your life of faith?

PRAYERS OF HOPE & HEALING

Pray for people of all ages who are unable to love themselves, or take in God's love deeply enough, because of crippling experiences of shame.

PRAYER FOR TODAY

O God, you love me just as I am, and you are able to use even my failure or falling as a window into your mercy. Thank you. Amen.

NOTES

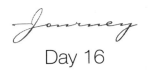

Day 16

JESUS REASSURES US, SAYING "I am the ground of your beseeching."
For it is the most impossible thing . . . that we should seek mercy and
grace and not have it. For everything which our good Lord makes us to
beseech he himself has ordained for us from all eternity. So here we may
see that our beseeching is not the cause of the goodness and grace which
he gives us, but his own goodness. . . . [T]he fruit and end of our prayer
. . . is to be united and like to our Lord in all things. . . . [T]his is the
Lord's will, that our prayer and trust be both equally generous. For if we
do not trust as much as we pray, we do not pay full honor to our Lord
in our prayer, and also we impede and hurt ourselves; and the reason is,
as I believe, that we do not truly know that our Lord is the ground from
which our prayer springs, and also because we do not know that it is
given to us by grace from his love.

BIBLICAL WISDOM

*Ask, and it will be given you; search, and you will find; knock, and the door will
be opened for you.* Matthew 7:7

SILENCE FOR MEDITATION

QUESTIONS TO PONDER

- Julian asserts that even our praying comes from Jesus' beckoning, not our
  own initiative. How does this correspond to your faith community's teaching about prayer?
- Do you agree that the fruit and end of our prayer is to be united to and
  become like Jesus in all things? If so, how does this shape your prayer? If
  not, what do you think is the fruit or goal of prayer?
- According to Julian, prayer and trust go together. What differences do you
  see between prayer that is trustful and prayer that is not?

PSALM FRAGMENT

You who live in the shelter of the Most High,
who abide in the shadow of the Almighty,
will say to the LORD, "My refuge and my fortress;
my God, in whom I trust." Psalm 91:1-2

JOURNAL REFLECTIONS

- Julian writes, "If we do not trust as much as we pray, we do not pay full honor to our Lord . . . and also we impede and hurt ourselves." Are there ways such fear and lack of trust "impede and hurt" you too? Explain. What would help deepen your trust in God?
- Do you sense a longing for more depth in prayer? If so, write about your longing, then talk to a friend or spiritual advisor about how you might respond to this longing.
- "The fruit and end of our prayer . . . is to be united and like to our Lord in all things." Write about any ways in which you sense the Spirit moving in your prayer to unite you to Christ and make you more like him.

PRAYERS OF HOPE & HEALING

Pray for those who struggle with trust: victims of trauma or betrayal. Pray for those who abuse others' trust, perhaps out of some violation in their own past experience.

PRAYER FOR TODAY

Lord Jesus, you are the source of all my praying, and the means of its being heard, and the goal toward which it draws me. Unite me fully to yourself, today and always. Amen.

NOTES

Day 17

But still our trust is often not complete, because we are not sure that God hears us . . . for often we are as barren and dry after our prayers as we were before. [Here Jesus says]: Pray wholeheartedly, though you may feel nothing, though you may see nothing, yes, though you think that you could not, for in dryness and in barrenness, in sickness and in weakness, then is your prayer most pleasing to me. [W]e ought to pray . . . that he may rule us and guide us to his glory in this life, and bring us to his bliss. . . . So he means us to see that he does it and to pray for it. For . . . if we pray and do not see that he does it, it makes us depressed and doubting. . . . And if we see that he does it and do not pray, we do not do our duty. . . . It is our Lord's will that we pray for everything which he has ordained to do, either in particular or in general. And so I saw that when we see the need for us to pray, then our Lord God is following us, helping our desire.

⌐

Biblical Wisdom

Then Jesus told them a parable about their need to pray always and not to lose heart. Luke 18:1

Silence for Meditation

Questions to Ponder

- Julian is addressing the experience of dryness or barrenness in prayer. What does your faith community believe about such dryness? Do you think that dryness in prayer reflects on the faith and commitment of the one who prays? Explain.
- Julian teaches that we are to pray for what the Lord "has [already] ordained to do." What do you think God has ordained to do? Does this mean we shouldn't pray for other things we long for?
- How does prayer itself help shape our desires to mirror God's desires?

Psalm Fragment

O Lord, I call to you;
   my rock, do not be deaf to my cry;
lest, if you do not hear me,
   I become like those who go down to the pit. . . .
You, Lord, are my strength and my shield;
   my heart trusts in you,
and I have been helped;
   so my heart exults, and with my song I give thanks to you. Psalm 28:1, 7

Journal Reflections

- Write about your own experiences of dryness in prayer. How do you handle such dryness?
- The sense of God's silence or absence can be disturbing if not frightening. If you have had such an experience, write a psalm to God expressing how you feel and respond when God seems silent or absent.
- Julian says that prayer is to ask for what is already happening: for God's mercy and grace to be poured out in your life and all things. How might this insight change your prayer?

Prayers of Hope & Healing

Pray for those who experience only God's absence in their praying, who doubt that there is any listener to their hearts.

Prayer for Today

O Holy One, you desire fullness of life for all creatures. Help me trust your will for my life and pray today for its unfolding in me. Amen.

Notes

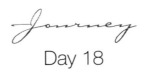

Day 18

BUT WHEN OUR COURTEOUS LORD of his special grace shows himself to our soul, we have what we desire, and then for that time we do not see what more we should pray for, but all our intention and all our powers are wholly directed to contemplating him. And as I see it, this is an exalted and imperceptible prayer; for the whole reason why we pray is to be united into the vision and contemplation of him to whom we pray . . . with so much sweetness and delight in him that we cannot pray at all except as he moves us at the time. . . . And then we can do no more than contemplate him and rejoice, with a great and compelling desire to be wholly united into him, and attend to his motion and rejoice in his love and delight in his goodness. . . . And [ultimately] we shall all come into our Lord, knowing ourselves clearly and wholly possessing God, and we shall all be endlessly hidden in God, truly seeing and wholly feeling, and hearing him spiritually and delectably smelling him and sweetly tasting him. And there we shall see God face to face, familiarly and wholly.

BIBLICAL WISDOM

Beloved, we are God's children now; what we will be has not yet been revealed. What we do know is this: when he is revealed, we will be like him, for we will see him as he is. 1 John 3:2

SILENCE FOR MEDITATION

QUESTIONS TO PONDER

- Julian states that the "whole reason" we pray is to obtain the "vision and contemplation" of Jesus. Do you agree? Why or why not? Make a list of the many reasons that you and others pray. How would you rank your list in order of importance?
- Julian's describes union with Christ as full of "so much sweetness and delight in him that we cannot pray at all except as he moves us at the time."

Is your faith community open to conversations about such intimate experiences of God? What are the gifts or dangers of such self-disclosure?

- In the next-to-last sentence of her writing above, Julian describes a glimpse of heaven, full of sensory images of intimacy with God. Read this sentence slowly. Which of her images moves you most? Explain.

PSALM FRAGMENT

"Come," my heart says, "seek [God's] face!"
   Your face, LORD, do I seek.
   Do not hide your face from me. Psalm 27:8-9

JOURNAL REFLECTIONS

- Have you had an experience similar to Julian's in which you have been given a vision of Christ or God? If so, describe the experience in your journal. How did it change you? What did you learn? If not, how would you imagine such an experience?
- Julian speaks of union with God as the great and compelling desire of the soul. Is this the desire that underlies your prayer or are there other desires that move you to pray? Explain.
- Where do you find the face of God? What characterizes it? In what ways (if at all) do you pray that your own face might better reflect God's face?

PRAYERS OF HOPE & HEALING

Pray for those who are ashamed of their faces and do not see the image of God reflected in themselves. Pray for those who attack or deny the face of God in others.

PRAYER FOR TODAY

Lord Jesus, in you we see God's face shining with love. Come let me see you face to face in my life today. Amen.

NOTES

IN GOD THERE CAN BE no anger. In all [my] contemplation it was necessary to see and know that we are sinners and commit many evil deeds which we ought to forsake, and leave many good deeds undone which we ought to do, so that we deserve pain, blame and wrath. And despite all this I saw truly that our Lord was never angry, and never will be. Because he is God, he is good, he is truth, he is love, he is peace; and his power, his wisdom, his charity and his unity do not allow him to be angry. For I saw no wrath except on [our] side, and he forgives that in us, for wrath is nothing else but a perversity and an opposition to peace and to love. And it comes from a lack of power or a lack of wisdom or a lack of goodness, and lack is not in God, but it is on our side. For we through sin and wretchedness have in us a wrath and a constant opposition to peace and to love; and he revealed that very often in his lovely look of compassion and pity.

BIBLICAL WISDOM

*Let the wicked forsake their way, and the unrighteous their thoughts; let them
     return to the LORD, that he may have mercy on them,
     and to our God, for he will abundantly pardon.
For my thoughts are not your thoughts,
     nor are your ways my ways, says the LORD.
For as the heavens are higher than the earth,
     so are my ways higher than your ways
     and my thoughts than your thoughts.* Isaiah 55:7-9

SILENCE FOR MEDITATION

QUESTIONS TO PONDER

• Julian asserts that there is no anger in God—none. Is this the way you experience God? Explain. How, if at all, does your faith community speak about anger in God?

- Why do you think Julian sees that it is "necessary to see and know that we are sinners" if in the end it turns out there is no anger in God? Can God motivate us to repent apart from wrath? Explain.
- Julian teaches that wrath is a human reality projected onto God. Do you agree? Why or why not? How do you think God's ways transcend our ways?

PSALM FRAGMENT

Be still before the LORD and wait patiently.
Do not be provoked by the one who prospers,
the one who succeeds in evil schemes.
Refrain from anger, leave rage alone;
do not be provoked; it leads only to evil. Psalm 37: 7-8 (ELW)

JOURNAL REFLECTIONS

- Write about your image of God. How do you see God? What are God's characteristics? How do these correspond to human characteristics? Explain.
- If God's "wrath" is a *human* projection and not part of God's own nature, does this change the image of God you grew up with? Explain. Talk to God about this.
- What feelings, thoughts, or behaviors of yours (if any) are you afraid God is angry about? Write about this. Imagine Jesus directing to you that "lovely look of compassion and pity" Julian sees him giving even (or especially) in "sin and wretchedness."

PRAYERS OF HOPE & HEALING:

Pray for those consumed by their own or others' anger: victims and aggressors, children and adults caught in abusive situations, persons living in situations of entrenched or corrosive injustice.

PRAYER FOR TODAY

O God, your ways are not our ways. Make me your vessel of hope and release for those caught in helplessness. Amen.

NOTES

Day 20

GOOD LORD, I SEE IN you that you are very truth, and I know truly that we sin grievously all day and are very blameworthy; and I can neither reject my knowledge of this truth, nor see that any kind of blame is shown to us. How can this be? For I know by the ordinary teaching of Holy Church and by my own feeling that the blame of our sins continually hangs upon us. . . . This then [caused me] astonishment, that I saw our Lord God showing no more blame to us than if we were as pure and as holy as the angels are in heaven. . . . I [felt] great fear and perplexity, thinking that if I were to take it that we are not sinners and not blameworthy, it seems as if I should err and fail to recognize the truth. And if it be true that we are sinners and blameworthy, good Lord, how can it then be that I cannot see this truth in you, who are my God, my maker in whom I desire to see all truth?

BIBLICAL WISDOM

The LORD does not see as mortals see; they look on the outward appearance, but the LORD looks on the heart. 1 Samuel 16:7b

SILENCE FOR MEDITATION

QUESTIONS TO PONDER

- Julian's vision that there is no anger in God conflicts both with what she has been taught by the church and her fear of God's anger at her sin. Has it ever happened to you that your experience of God diverged from your faith community's teaching or your upbringing? Explain.
- Julian's experience of this conflict causes her "great fear and perplexity." If you have experienced conflicts between your spiritual experience and the church's teaching, how have you handled them?

- What helps the Christian community grapple with new insights like Julian's? What ought to distinguish Christian revelation—however radical it may initially appear—from misguided or harmful teachings? How is the truth of a new insight tested over time?

PSALM FRAGMENT

Search me, O God, and know my heart;
  test me and know my thoughts.
See if there is any wicked way in me,
  and lead me in the way everlasting. Psalm 139: 23-24

JOURNAL REFLECTIONS

- Make a list in your journal of questions arising from your experiences of life and God that you long to have answers for. (Reflect deeply. Remember that some questions are hidden in dreams, compulsions, fears, hungers.)
- Do you suppress any of your heart's questions for fear they might "threaten" God or the authorities of your faith or upbringing? Explain. If you answered yes, what might help you give expression to these "threatening" questions?
- Write a poem or prayer, create a collage, draw a picture, or choose a piece of music that expresses as best you can the questions you are afraid to ask of God or yourself. Pray your questions. What surprises you in what you create or hear? What emerges in you as you pray the questions?

PRAYERS OF HOPE & HEALING

Pray for those who help people give voice to their authentic questions before God: teachers, therapists, clergypersons, spiritual directors, friends of the heart. Pray for all who have no one to hear them. Pray for ears to hear the cries of the earth and the poor, even when they seem to threaten us.

PRAYER FOR TODAY

O God, you hear the questions I am afraid to ask. Give me courage to trust you with the insights, fears, and dreams that challenge my life's status quo. Amen.

NOTES

I SAW . . . a lord and a servant. . . . [The lord] looks on his servant very lovingly and sweetly and mildly. He sends him to . . . do his will. Not only does the servant go, but he dashes off and runs at great speed, loving to do his lord's will. And soon he falls into a dell and is greatly injured; and then he groans and moans and tosses about and writhes, but he cannot rise or help himself in any way. And . . . the greatest hurt which I saw him in was lack of consolation, for he could not turn his face to look on his loving lord. . . . [This] is a great sorrow and a cruel suffering to him, for he neither sees clearly his loving lord, who is so meek and mild to him, nor does he truly see what he himself is in the sight of his loving lord. And I know well that when these two things are wisely and truly seen, we shall gain rest and peace . . . by God's plentiful grace. . . . And the loving regard which [the lord] kept constantly on his servant, and especially when he fell . . . could melt our hearts for love and break them in two for joy.

࿐

BIBLICAL WISDOM

Here is my servant, whom I uphold,
  my chosen, in whom my soul delights. Isaiah 42:1a

SILENCE FOR MEDITATION

QUESTIONS TO PONDER

- Julian experiences this vision of a lord and servant as the beginning of God's response to her question in yesterday's excerpt (how our "falling" is seen by God). How do you and/or your faith community understand the language of "the fall" as a metaphor for human sin?
- Is the servant's situation (injured, groaning, unable to get up or help himself, unable to see his lord's face) similar to your own experience of sin? Are there ways it differs from that experience? Explain.

- Julian asserts that when we, like the servant, are restored to see our loving lord clearly, and to see ourselves wisely and truly as we are in God's sight, then "we shall gain rest and peace." Do you sense God at work toward these goals in you? Explain.

PSALM FRAGMENT

The LORD is near to the brokenhearted,
and saves those whose spirits are crushed . . . .
O LORD, you redeem the life of your servants,
and those who put their trust in you will not be punished.
Psalm 34:18, 22 (ELW)

JOURNAL REFLECTIONS

- Meditate on Julian's final sentence in her writing, above. What keeps you from being able to imagine, see, trust, or abide all the time in the heart-melting, rapturous love of God for you?
- An effect of the fall is the inability to see ourselves clearly as God sees us. Write about how you see yourself in the sight of your loving God.
- Spend time simply resting in God's endless "loving regard" for you and us all. What feelings are evoked? Try to stay there all day. Tomorrow too. And the next day.

PRAYERS OF HOPE & HEALING

Pray for those with blind eyes and those with blind hearts. Pray for all who care for those with any kind of blindness. Pray in gratitude for all that truly helps us to see and for the astonishing miracle of being alive at all.

PRAYER FOR TODAY

O God, when I fall you see me and keep loving me. Help me abide always in your love. Amen.

NOTES

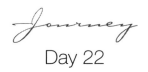

Day 22

IN THE SERVANT [SEE DAY 21's reading] is comprehended the second person of the Trinity, and in the servant is comprehended Adam, that is to say all [persons]. And therefore . . . when I say "the servant," that means Christ's humanity, which is the true Adam. When Adam fell, God's Son fell; because of the true union which was made in heaven, God's Son could not be separated from Adam. . . . Adam fell from life to death, into the valley of this wretched world, and after that into hell. God's Son fell with Adam, into the valley of the womb of the maiden who was the fairest daughter of Adam, and that was to excuse Adam from blame in heaven and on earth; and powerfully he brought him out of hell. For all [human]kind which will be saved by the sweet Incarnation and the Passion of Christ, all is Christ's humanity, for he is the head and we are his members . . . for Jesus is in all who will be saved, and all who will be saved are in Jesus, and all is of the love of God. . . . [For] I saw that only pain blames and punishes, and our courteous Lord [is] . . . always kindly disposed to the soul.

BIBLICAL WISDOM

For since death came through a human being, the resurrection of the dead has also come through a human being; for as all die in Adam, so all will be made alive in Christ. 1 Corinthians 15:21-22

SILENCE FOR MEDITATION

QUESTIONS TO PONDER

- What do you think it means that the servant in Julian's parable represents both Christ and "Adam," a metaphor for all humanity? Is this a comfort for you? Why or why not?
- The vision of our union with Jesus' humanity is at the heart of Julian's conviction that there is no divine wrath. That is, Julian sees Jesus'

crucifixion—his deepest "fall" from heaven—embracing our fall and joining us to his resurrection. Does this vision of how Jesus saves us make sense to you? Explain.

- How does Julian's insight that we are all united in Christ's humanity shape your faith community's approach to issues of social justice? Or the failings, shortcomings, sins, and sinners of our world?

Psalm Fragment

O LORD my God, I cried to you for help,
  and you have healed me.
O LORD, you brought up my soul from Sheol,
  restored me to life from among those gone down to the Pit. Psalm 30:2-3

Journal Reflections

- In poetic and metaphorical images, Julian declares that Christ's incarnation and passion bring "Adam" (humanity) out of hell. Reflect on your life. With "hell" as a metaphor for the bondage of sin, in what (if any) ways do you long to be released from hell? If you need to be brought out of "hell," talk to Jesus about it. Perhaps you could write a prayer to him.
- Could Julian's insight that God neither blames nor punishes help you to tell which of your inner voices are of God and which are not? Explain.
- Reflect on Julian's insight that you share in Christ's humanity. What are the implications of this insight for the way you understand and live your life? For the way you approach your death?

Prayers of Hope & Healing

Pray for those who risk their lives descending into hell for the sake of others: firefighters, police officers, soldiers, social workers, whistle-blowers, disaster relief workers. Pray for those who see no way out.

Prayer for Today

Lord Jesus, you come to embrace me even in my fallenness and to restore me to abundance of life. Thank you. Amen.

Notes

AND THUS I SAW THAT he wants us to know that he takes the falling of any creature who will be saved no harder than he took the falling of Adam, who, we know, was endlessly loved and safely protected in all the time of his need, and now is blissfully restored in great and surpassing joys. For our Lord God is so good, so gentle and so courteous that he can never assign final failure to those in whom he will always be blessed and praised. I saw and understood very surely that in each soul which will be saved there is a godly will which never assented to sin nor ever will. Therefore our Lord wants us to know . . . that we have all this blessed will whole and safe in our Lord Jesus Christ, because every nature with which heaven will be filled had of necessity . . . to be so joined and united in him that in it a substance was kept which could never and should never be parted from him.

BIBLICAL WISDOM

I do not understand my own actions. For I do not do what I want, but I do the very thing I hate. . . . Now if I do what I do not want, it is no longer I that do it, but sin that dwells within me. . . . For I delight in the law of God in my inmost self, but I see in my members another law at war with the law of my mind, making me captive to the law of sin that dwells in my members. Romans 7:15, 20, 22-23

SILENCE FOR MEDITATION

QUESTIONS TO PONDER

- Julian asserts that Christians have a "godly will," the core of our soul united to Jesus Christ and held in him, that "never assented to sin nor ever will." How does this compare to St. Paul's experience of his "inmost self" loving God and resisting the sin he commits? How does it compare to your experience?

- Does this assertion help you to understand why Julian believes that there is no blaming in God? Explain.
- Do you think all people are good at their core? Explain.

PSALM FRAGMENT

O LORD, you have searched me and known me.
You know when I sit down and when I rise up;
*   you discern my thoughts from far away . . .*
Even before a word is on my tongue,
*   O LORD, you know it completely.* Psalm 139:1-2, 4

JOURNAL REFLECTIONS

- How do you think of yourself—at your core—as sinful or good, as ugly or beautiful, as unlovable or lovable, as shameful or worthy? Explain. How, if at all, does Julian's vision begin to change (or affirm) your self-image?
- Journal about where your self-image comes from. Why do you think about yourself the way you do?
- Look at a favorite icon, image, or picture of Jesus, preferably one where he is gazing at you. If you don't have a picture like this, imagine Jesus' eyes holding yours. Write about the "you" he sees. Tell him how it feels to be seen by him, and linger in his love.

PRAYERS OF HOPE AND HEALING

Pray for all who are unable to love themselves or see their own beauty and priceless worth.

PRAYER FOR TODAY

Lord Jesus, you love me through and through, and keep me held safe in you forever. Help me see myself and all I meet today through your eyes of love. Amen.

NOTES

Day 24

AND THEN OUR GOOD LORD . . . showed me my soul in the midst of my heart. I saw the soul as wide as if it were an endless citadel, and also as if it were a blessed kingdom, and from the state which I saw in it, I understood that it is a fine city. In the midst of that city sits our Lord Jesus Christ, true God and true man, . . . and he rules and guards heaven and earth and everything that is. The place which Jesus takes in our soul he will nevermore vacate, for in us is his home of homes, and it is the greatest delight for him to dwell there. Greatly ought we to rejoice that God dwells in our soul; and more greatly ought we to rejoice that our soul dwells in God. Our soul is created to be God's dwelling place, and the dwelling of our soul is God, who is uncreated. Marvelous and splendid is the place where the Lord dwells; and therefore he wants us promptly to attend to the touching of his grace, rejoicing more in his unbroken love than sorrowing over our frequent failings.

⌒

BIBLICAL WISDOM

And I saw the holy city, the new Jerusalem, coming down out of heaven from God, prepared as a bride adorned for her husband. And I heard a loud voice from the throne saying,
> *"See, the home of God is among mortals.*
> *He will dwell with them as their God;*
> *they will be his peoples,*
> *and God himself will be with them."* Revelation 21:2-3

SILENCE FOR MEDITATION

QUESTIONS TO PONDER

- Describe the differences you might find between a faith community that focuses on God's unbroken love and a faith community that focuses on sorrow for human failings.
- Julian states: "Our soul is created to be God's dwelling place." What do you think this means?

- Julian states that we are Jesus' "home of homes." In what ways might our bodies and lives reflect Jesus' endless delighted dwelling within us?

PSALM FRAGMENT

How lovely is your dwelling place,
  O LORD of hosts!
My soul longs, indeed it faints
  for the courts of the LORD;
my heart and my flesh sing for joy
  to the living God. Psalm 84:1-2

JOURNAL REFLECTIONS

- The soul as a city, or as a house with various rooms and levels, is a frequent image in dreams. If you have ever had such a dream of your soul, record it in your journal. Consider starting a dream journal in which you can record and reflect on your dreams.
- According to Julian, because Jesus dwells within us we should "attend to the touching of his grace." Record in your journal any times or places or circumstances when you felt within you the touch of Jesus' grace.
- How would you describe the "city" that is your soul? Is it gorgeous and expansive? Warm and cozy? Is it fragile, with holes in the walls? There's no right or wrong image; draw or write what springs to mind, and open any feelings or questions this stirs to God.

PRAYERS OF HOPE & HEALING

Pray for those who live in cities around the world, especially those most at risk: immigrants or refugees, those without adequate housing, those in poverty. Pray with gratitude for the gifts of cities and their culture and history.

PRAYER FOR TODAY

O God, you dwell at the heart of each human being, each person an entire city of complexity and beauty. Show me the grace of my own architecture and that of others. Amen.

NOTES

AND IN THIS HE REVEALED the delight that he has in the creation of [our] soul; for as well as the Father could create a creature and as well as the Son could create a creature, so well did the Holy Spirit want [our] spirit to be created, and so it was done. And therefore the blessed Trinity rejoices without end in the creation of [our] soul, for it saw without beginning what would delight it without end. . . . For I saw in the same revelation that if the blessed Trinity could have created [our] soul any better, any fairer, any nobler than it was created, the Trinity would not have been fully pleased with the creation of [our] soul. But because it made [our] soul as beautiful, as good, as precious a creature as it could make, therefore the blessed Trinity is fully pleased without end in the creation of [our] soul. For our soul sits in God in true rest, and our soul stands in God in sure strength, and our soul is naturally rooted in God in endless love.

BIBLICAL WISDOM

But now thus says the LORD, he who created you, O Jacob, he who formed you, O Israel:
   Do not fear, for I have redeemed you;
   I have called you by name, you are mine. Isaiah 43:1

SILENCE FOR MEDITATION

QUESTIONS TO PONDER

- If you could have been created "better," that would mean God had done inadequate work creating you, which is impossible. Do you truly believe God created you? And continues to create you? If so, what impact does that belief have on who and how you are?
- Again, Julian uses Trinitarian language. Do you find the concept of the Trinity helpful in understanding God's creation? Why or why not?
- When God looks at the whole creation, and every human being, and describes it as "very good," what does that imply for the way we treat our bodies? One another? The planet itself?

Psalm Fragment

My frame was not hidden from you,
when I was being made in secret,
intricately woven in the depths of the earth.
Your eyes beheld my unformed substance.
In your book were written
all the days that were formed for me,
when none of them as yet existed. Psalm 139:15-16

Journal Reflections

- Like the psalmist, you were "intricately woven" by God with exquisite care in your creation. Meditate on the unfathomable complexity of your body, your unique architecture of flesh and spirit and heart and mind, all crafted by God. Record your thoughts and feelings.
- According to Julian, sitting, standing, walking, or resting, you abide in God. This is how you are created. Try sitting in silence for five or ten minutes today (longer if you are accustomed to silence), meditating on the unvarnished *reality* of you—the fact that *you are* and that *you are in God.* Record your meditation in your journal.
- According to Julian, in first imagining *your* existence, the whole Trinity "saw without beginning what would delight it without end," and "rejoices without end" in your creation. Are you able to accept God's love and delight in you? Why or why not?

Prayers of Hope & Healing

Pray for all natural creatures and ecosystems threatened by human greed and destruction. Pray that those who are greedy and destructive may glimpse their own created goodness and the goodness of all others.

Prayer for Today

Holy Spirit, you breathe in all living things. Help me rest today in the love by which you are endlessly creating me. Amen.

Notes

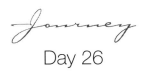

Day 26

THOUGH OUR LORD REVEALED TO me that I . . . [will] sin, by me is understood everyone. And in this I conceived a gentle fear, and in answer to this our Lord said: I protect you very safely. This word was said with more love and assurance of protection for my soul than I can or may tell. For just as it was first revealed to me that I should sin, so was consolation revealed—assurance of protection for all my fellow Christians. What can make me love my fellow Christians more than to see in God that he loves all who will be saved, all of them as it were one soul? For we cannot be blessedly saved until we are truly in peace and in love, for that is our salvation. [There we will be] wholly contented with God and with all his works and with all his judgments, and loving and content with ourselves and with our fellow Christians and with everything which God loves, as is pleasing to love. And God's goodness does this in us.

BIBLICAL WISDOM

The glory that you have given me I have given them, so that they may be one, as we are one, I in them and you in me, that they may become completely one, so that the world may know that you have sent me and have loved them even as you have loved me. John 17:22-23

SILENCE FOR MEDITATION

QUESTIONS TO PONDER

- Julian declares: "What can make me love my fellow Christians more than to see in God that he loves all who will be saved, all of them as it were one soul?" How might this insight shape our relationships with those we have considered our enemies?
- This passage ends with a reflection on contentment in God. Can you think of a time when you were "wholly contented with God," yourself, and others? If so, describe it. If not, why not?

- Julian states that salvation is being "wholly contented with God . . . and loving and content with ourselves and with our fellow Christians and with everything which God loves." How does this square with the way you and your faith community understand salvation?

PSALM FRAGMENT

The LORD is my chosen portion and my cup;
   you hold my lot.
The boundary lines have fallen for me in pleasant places;
   I have a goodly heritage. . . .
You show me the path of life.
   In your presence there is fullness of joy;
   in your right hand are pleasures forevermore. Psalm 16:5-6, 11

JOURNAL REFLECTIONS

- Julian is greatly moved by Jesus' promise, even in her sin: "I protect you very safely." What, if any, sins or dangers do you face from which you wish to ask Jesus to protect you? Ask him.
- Julian suggests that it is not outward characteristics we have in common, but precisely our shared fragility, vulnerability to sin, and need for Jesus' protection, that unites us to others. Does that ring true? Why or why not?
- Julian seems to say that sin is inevitable. How does this make you feel?

PRAYERS OF HOPE & HEALING

Pray for those who may find it difficult to be content: the hungry or starving, those in acute or chronic pain, and victims of injustice, poverty, or crime. Pray for those whose lack of contentment derives from having too much work, too little love, or alienation from the earth and its beauty.

PRAYER FOR TODAY

O God, you long to make me wholly content in you. Help me place my trust in your love, which will never fail or forsake me. Amen.

NOTES

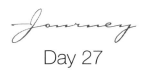

Day 27

I CONTEMPLATED THE WORK OF all the blessed Trinity, in which contemplation I saw and understood these three properties: the property of the fatherhood, and the property of the motherhood, and the property of the Lordship in one God. . . . As to the first, I saw and understood that the high might of the Trinity is our Father, and the deep wisdom of the Trinity is our Mother, and the great love of the Trinity is our Lord; and all these we have in nature and in our substantial creation. . . . As truly as God is our Father, so truly is God our Mother, and he revealed that in everything. . . . I understand three ways of contemplating motherhood in God. The first is the foundation of our nature's creation; the second is his taking of our nature, where the motherhood of grace begins; the third is the motherhood at work. And in that, by the same grace, everything is penetrated, in length and in breadth, in height and in depth without end; and it is all one love.

⌒

BIBLICAL WISDOM

I pray that you may have the power to comprehend, with all the saints, what is the breadth and length and height and depth, and to know the love of Christ that surpasses knowledge, so that you may be filled with all the fullness of God.
Ephesians 3:18-19

SILENCE FOR MEDITATION

QUESTIONS TO PONDER

- Have you ever thought of God as our Mother? Explain. In your faith community, what images or names are used for God in worship, prayer, teaching, or devotion?
- Christian tradition, including Jesus' teaching, has given much more weight to the image of God as Father than Mother. What qualities do you associate with God as "father"? With God as "mother"? Which do you prefer? Why?

- Julian uses mother imagery for all three Persons of the Trinity, but most consistently connects it with Jesus. Why do you think she does this?

PSALM FRAGMENT

O LORD, my heart is not lifted up,
my eyes are not raised too high;
I do not occupy myself with things
too great and too marvelous for me.
But I have calmed and quieted my soul,
like a weaned child with its mother;
my soul is like the weaned child that is with me. Psalm 131:1-2

JOURNAL REFLECTIONS

- Think about your own mother (or stepmother or foster mother). What characteristics come to mind when you think of her? Does (or did) your mother uniquely reflect the face of God to you? If so, how? How does thinking of God as Mother transcend, complement, or help to heal your experience of your own mother's limitations? Speak to God of the thoughts and feelings this exercise evokes.
- What similar patterns of revelation and healing do you experience when you think of God as Father in relation to your own father?
- "As truly as God is our Father, so truly is God our Mother." Try addressing God with whichever parental image is less familiar. How does it feel to pray with this name?

PRAYERS OF HOPE & HEALING

Pray for mothers and fathers and all whose love and limits are shaping children's earliest conceptions of God. Pray for children who do not have adequate parenting.

PRAYER FOR TODAY

O God, my Mother, my Father, thank you for creating me in your image and for loving me in all the ways I most deeply need. Amen.

NOTES

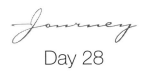

JESUS CHRIST, WHO OPPOSES GOOD to evil, is our true Mother. We have our being from him, where the foundation of motherhood begins. . . . We know that all our mothers bear us for pain and for death. . . . But our true Mother Jesus . . . alone bears us for joy and for endless life, blessed may he be. So he carries us within him in love and travail, until the full time when he wanted to suffer the sharpest thorns and cruel pains . . . and at the last he died. And when he had finished, and had so borne us for bliss, still all this could not satisfy his wonderful love. . . . To the property of motherhood belong nature, love, wisdom and knowledge, and this is God. For though it may be that our bodily bringing to birth is only little, humble and simple in comparison with our spiritual bringing to birth, still it is he who does it in the creatures by whom it is done. . . . And in our spiritual bringing to birth he uses more tenderness, without any comparison, in protecting us. . . . And from this sweet and gentle operation he will neither cease or desist, until all his beloved children are born and brought to birth.

BIBLICAL WISDOM

But when they came to Jesus and saw that he was already dead, they did not break his legs. Instead, one of the soldiers pierced his side with a spear, and at once blood and water came out. John 19:33-34

SILENCE FOR MEDITATION

QUESTIONS TO PONDER

- Julian uses the metaphor of pregnancy in talking about Jesus as mother. As a human mother bears her baby as it grows toward birth, Jesus too bears us in his Body toward our birth in the Spirit. Have you ever felt "borne" by God? Explain.
- The labor of giving birth is excruciating for human mothers and for Jesus. Julian sees Jesus' passion and death as his extraordinary new birthing of

us, in the divine blood and water (John 1:12, 19:34). How do you react to this image? Does it change the way you see the cross? Explain.

- To be born of water and the Spirit (John 3:5) is an image of Christian baptism. How do you or your faith community understand baptism and its regenerative "birthing" power?

PSALM FRAGMENT

Upon you I have leaned from my birth;
*   it was you who took me from my mother's womb.*
My praise is continually of you. Psalm 71:6

JOURNAL REFLECTIONS

- Write down any stories you know about your mother's pregnancy with you or your birth. Do these stories help you to understand Julian's metaphor of Jesus as mother? Explain. Write about any experiences of spiritual rebirth you have had.
- If you have been pregnant, you may grasp in your own body the power of Julian's image of Jesus' being pregnant with us and giving us birth. What does your experience of pregnancy or giving birth reveal about Jesus' ongoing bearing and motherhood of you?
- All of us, whether or not we have been pregnant, were once babies held in the womb: an experience of safety, warmth, protection, and nourishment. Meditate on being borne in God's nurturing womb. What feelings or reactions does this evoke?

PRAYERS OF HOPE & HEALING

Pray for all women in or preparing for childbirth; for all who will die today (women or newborns) in childbirth; in gratitude for the miracle of conception, gestation, and birth.

PRAYER FOR TODAY

O God, in you I was conceived and born. Thank you for Jesus' labor to make me your child by water and his maternal blood in the Spirit. Amen.

NOTES

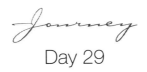
THE MOTHER CAN GIVE HER child to suck of her milk, but our precious Mother Jesus can feed us with himself, and does, most courteously and most tenderly, with the blessed sacrament, which is the precious food of true life; and with all the sweet sacraments he sustains us most mercifully and graciously. . . . [And he says]: All the health and the life of the sacraments, all the power and the grace of my Word, all the goodness which is ordained in Holy Church for you, I am he. . . . The mother can lay her child tenderly to her breast, but our tender Mother Jesus can lead us easily into his blessed breast through his sweet open side, and show us there a part of the godhead and of the joys of heaven, with inner certainty of endless bliss. And that he revealed [in saying]: "See how I love you!" This fair lovely word "mother" is so sweet and so kind in itself that it cannot truly be said of anyone or to anyone except of him and to him who is the true Mother of life and of all things.

ↄ

BIBLICAL WISDOM

Like newborn infants, long for the pure, spiritual milk, so that by it you may grow into salvation. 1 Peter 2:2

SILENCE FOR MEDITATION

QUESTIONS TO PONDER

- The gift of sustenance is crucial to motherhood: the mother providing milk for her newborn from her own body, created from her own blood. Julian sees breast feeding as an image of the Eucharist, our nourishment by Jesus' own body and blood. What feelings does this image stir in you?
- What does your faith community teach about Holy Communion? How (if at all) does Julian's metaphor of the sacrament as Jesus' maternal milk

connect with your belief? How might seeing the Eucharist as Mother's milk recast your view of Jesus' real presence in the sacrament?

- As with many Christian mystics, Julian sees the wound in Jesus' side not as merely a mark of his torment, but as a place of access to the depths of his body, his heart, his love. What wounds—of Jesus, of your own, or of others—have opened the depths of Jesus' heart and love to you?

PSALM FRAGMENT

Taste and see that the LORD is good;
*   happy are they who take refuge in God!* Psalm 34:8 (ELW)

JOURNAL REFLECTIONS

- Julian asserts that, like newborns, we receive the spiritual milk given by our divine Mother to feed us. Where are the primary places or means by which God feeds you? Is your spiritual hunger satisfied, or are there places in you still yearning and hungering for God? Tell God about these.
- Consider a breast-feeding infant: held close, meeting the loving gaze of its mother, hungers filled, love given and received. Have you ever experienced such love from God? Let yourself pray with this image, and journal on your experience and feelings.
- "See how I love you!" Jesus says to Julian and to us all. Spend time in silent meditation, soaking up this love, repeating Jesus' words deep in your heart. Journal about the experience.

PRAYERS OF HOPE & HEALING

Pray for all breast-feeding mothers (human mothers and animals) and their babies; for those who are unable to nurse their children; for all who are starving for food or for love.

PRAYER FOR TODAY

Lord Jesus, thank you for feeding me with your own body and blood. Help me look into your eyes and trust that you love me completely. Amen.

NOTES

Day 30

OFTEN WHEN OUR FALLING AND our wretchedness are shown to us, we are so . . . greatly ashamed of ourselves that we scarcely know where we can put ourselves. But then our courteous Mother does not wish us to flee away, for nothing would be less pleasing to him; but he then wants us to behave like a child. For when it is distressed and frightened, it runs quickly to its mother; and if it can do no more, it calls to the mother for help with all its might. So he wants us [to cry out]: My kind Mother, my gracious Mother, my beloved Mother, have mercy on me. I have made myself filthy and unlike you, and I may not and cannot make it right except with your help and grace. . . . For the flood of mercy which is his dear blood and precious water is plentiful to make us fair and clean. . . . The sweet gracious hands of our Mother are ready and diligent about us. . . . It is his office to save us, it is his glory to do it, and it is his will that we know it; for he wants us to love him sweetly and trust in him meekly and greatly.

BIBLICAL WISDOM

How often have I desired to gather your children together as a hen gathers her brood under her wings. Luke 13:34b

SILENCE FOR MEDITATION

QUESTIONS TO PONDER

- When our sins or failings are revealed, we often want to hide: from ourselves, from others, and from God. What aspects of yourself do you find hardest to face, to show to others, or to open to God? Why?
- Despite our impulse to hide, Julian notes that "our courteous Mother does not wish us to flee, for nothing would be less pleasing to him." She invites us to run to God in trust instead. Could God in fact want to be with us even when we're ashamed of ourselves? Explain.

- Think of a time you have observed a wise mother or father embracing a filthy, disgraced, or needy child in great love. What was the effect on the child? On you watching? What do you see of God in such parents? Is this divine love for you too?

PSALM FRAGMENT

Look upon the LORD and be radiant,
And let not your faces be ashamed.
I cried in my affliction, and the LORD heard me
and saved me from all my troubles. Psalm 34:5-6 (ELW)

JOURNAL REFLECTIONS

- Earlier Julian connected the blood and water from Jesus' pierced side to our birth as children of God. Here the blood and water open a different baptismal image: cleansing, a veritable flood of mercy. Reflect on your life and ask God in your journal for any cleansing you need.
- Were you able to approach your mother in trust when you were hurt, afraid, or had done something wrong as a child? Are you able to open your feelings and desires to God and to approach God when you're ashamed of yourself? Write about these experiences.
- In the light of Jesus' great maternal love and mercy, write about what it would mean for you to "behave like a child."

PRAYERS OF HOPE & HEALING

Pray for children who do not have parents welcoming of their needs or limits; for all who are alienated from their parents or children. Pray for those preparing for the cleansing new birth of baptism.

PRAYER FOR TODAY

Lord Jesus, you welcome all who sin to find shelter under your wings. Draw me to yourself this day and teach me your ways of love. Amen.

NOTES

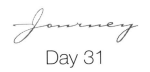

Day 31

BUT BECAUSE OF OUR OWN inconstancy, we often fall into sin. [Then] the prompting of our enemy and . . . our own folly and blindness . . . say: You know well that you are a wretch, a sinner and also unfaithful. . . . Often you promise our Lord that you will do better, and then you fall again into the same state, especially into sloth and wasting of time, for that, as I see it, is the beginning of sin. And this makes [us] afraid to appear before our courteous Lord. Thus it is our enemy who wants to retard us with his false suggestions of fear about our wretchedness. . . . For it is his purpose to make us so depressed and sad in this matter that we should forget the blessed contemplation of our everlasting friend. . . . So this is the remedy, that we acknowledge our wretchedness and flee to our Lord; for always, the more abased we are, the more profitable it is for us to touch him.

BIBLICAL WISDOM

The accuser of our comrades has been thrown down,
who accuses them day and night before our God.
But they have conquered him by the blood of the Lamb. Revelation 12:10c-11a

SILENCE FOR MEDITATION

QUESTIONS TO PONDER

- As we have seen, our trust in God can easily be derailed by the whisperings of fear and shame in us. Julian worries that she is "a wretch, a sinner and also unfaithful." What do the inner voices of attack seize on in accusing you? What terms of reproach do they use?
- To recognize that such attack comes not from God but from the "accuser" of our souls (Revelation 12) is the first step in resisting it. What is the difference between such destructive accusation and honest self-awareness of our sin?

- For Julian, "sloth and wasting of time" are root problems underlying much sin. Do you agree? Why or why not?

PSALM FRAGMENT

It is in vain to rise so early and go to bed so late;
vain, too, to eat the bread of toil;
for you, LORD, give sleep to your beloved. Psalm 127:2 (ELW)

JOURNAL REFLECTIONS

- Release from accusation comes when we are able to "acknowledge our wretchedness and flee to our Lord." Tell Jesus in your journal about any inner accusations that trouble you.
- Julian reassures us that "the more abased we are, the more profitable it is for us to touch [Jesus]." Have you touched Jesus in his contemporary Body, the church? Have you let others touch you?
- The psalmist writes that God "gives sleep to [the] beloved." Not only sloth but also overwork can be a sign of lack of trust in God. Do you tend to one extreme or the other? Explain.

PRAYERS OF HOPE & HEALING

Pray for those who have little or no loving human touch in their lives: many single or elderly people, those with contagious diseases, the "untouchables." Pray for those who are afraid of touch.

PRAYER FOR TODAY

Lord Jesus, you extend your heart and hand and Body to embrace me. Thank you that you welcome my touch too, today and always. Amen.

NOTES

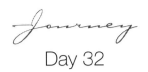

Day 32

AND WHEN WE FALL, QUICKLY he raises us up with his loving embrace and his gracious touch. And when we are strengthened by his sweet working, then we willingly choose him by his grace, that we shall be his servants and his lovers, constantly and forever. . . . And our falling is not evidence of divine negligence or lack of love. For we need to fall, and we need to see it; for if we did not fall we should not know how feeble and how wretched we are in ourselves, nor, too, should we know so completely the wonderful love of our Creator. . . . And by the experience of this falling we shall have a great and marvelous knowledge of love in God without end; for enduring and marvelous is that love which cannot and will not be broken because of offenses. . . . [Therefore] let us meekly recognize our weakness, knowing that we cannot stand for the twinkling of an eye except with the protection of grace, and let us reverently cling to God, trusting only in him.

BIBLICAL WISDOM

For by grace you have been saved through faith, and this is not your own doing; it is the gift of God—not the result of works, so that no one may boast.
Ephesians 2:8-9

SILENCE FOR MEDITATION

QUESTIONS TO PONDER

- Julian points out the value of falling. She claims "we need to fall" because it teaches us humility, our need for God, and the love of God. What do you think of this positive view of falling? How would your faith community respond to Julian's claim?
- What is the difference in your experience between a fall that brings humility and trust, as well as real pain, and one that brings only devastation or collapse?

- For Julian, we are totally dependent on grace. Do you agree? Why or why not?

PSALM FRAGMENT

My whole being clings to you;
your right hand holds me fast. Psalm 63:8 (ELW)

JOURNAL REFLECTIONS

- Throughout her visions, Julian is learning that falling (the experience of sin, of need, of brokenness) is no obstacle to God's grace and can in fact be precisely the place of the deepest experience of such grace. Write about whether or not this is also true of your experience.
- "Let us reverently cling to God." This is the faith that allows grace to save us: deep trust in God, willingness to be in need and be fully loved. What does faith mean to you?
- Trusting God from the core of our being is the vocation of a lifetime—and beyond. What helps (or perhaps forces) you to trust God completely? What aspects of your life, including your religious life, tend to impede such trust?

PRAYERS OF HOPE & HEALING

Pray for all people of faith, including those of different faiths, and for those who struggle to have any faith at all in the face of cynicism, poverty, or despair.

PRAYER FOR TODAY

Holy Spirit, breathe in me, that I may live this day trusting your power and love at work in all things. Amen.

NOTES

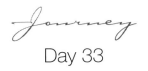
WHATEVER KINDS OF FEAR BE suggested to us other than reverent fear, though they appear disguised as holiness, they are not . . . ; and this is how they can be recognized apart. The fear that makes us hastily to flee from everything that is not good, and to fall into our Lord's breast, as the child into the mother's arms, with all our intention and with all our mind, knowing our feebleness and our great need, knowing his everlasting goodness and his blessed love, seeking only in him for salvation, cleaving to him with faithful trust, that fear which leads us in this direction is gentle and gracious and good and true; and all that is opposed to this is either wrong or mixed with wrong. So this is the remedy, to recognize them both and to refuse the wrong; for the natural attribute of fear which we have in this life by the grace-giving operation of the Holy Spirit will be the same in heaven before God, gentle, courteous, most sweet; and thus in love we shall be familiar and close to God, and in fear we shall be gentle and courteous to God, and both . . . in the same way.

BIBLICAL WISDOM

There is no fear in love, but perfect love casts out fear; for fear has to do with punishment, and whoever fears has not reached perfection in love. 1 John 4:18

SILENCE FOR MEDITATION

QUESTIONS TO PONDER

- Julian lived in a time of plague, war, famine, and need. She knew how people exploit others' fears to consolidate their own power or sell the assurance of God's protection. Where do you see people's fear being exploited under religious guise today?
- The opposite of a false fear-based conception of God is one grounded in grace. There's nothing to be afraid of; you don't have to cower before the

one who loves you endlessly from before your very creation, and in whom there is no wrath. Does this ring true for you? If so, in what ways? If not, why not?

- Do you or your faith community see a positive role for religious fear, awe, or mystery in the life of faith? Explain. Does Julian's language of "reverent fear" speak to you? Why or why not?

PSALM FRAGMENT

Fear the LORD, you saints of the LORD,
*   for those who fear the LORD lack nothing.* Psalm 34:9 (ELW)

JOURNAL REFLECTIONS

- What are you afraid of? What keeps you awake at night? What anxieties fill your daydreams or emerge in your nightmares? Write your worst fears as a prayer to God.
- Julian connects "reverent fear" with a profound sense of trust. Again she uses the image of a mother whom a child trusts completely, yet to whom the child also knows to listen closely and obey. How well does this image reflect your relationship with God? Explain.
- Martin Luther wrote that "we are to fear, love, and trust God above all things." Which of these comes most easily for you? Which is most difficult? Write about what you need in order to grow in all three.

PRAYERS OF HOPE & HEALING

Pray for those controlled by their fears, both rational and irrational. Pray for those being exploited by violence or social forces to keep them fearful. Pray for fear-mongers.

PRAYER FOR TODAY

Lord God, you banish fears and release me from the power of all that would bind me. Help me learn to fear, love, and trust you above all things. Amen.

NOTES

[OUR LORD] WANTS US TO see our wretchedness and meekly to acknowledge it; but he does not want us to remain there, or to be much occupied in self-accusation, nor does he want us to be too full of our own misery. But he wants us quickly to attend to him, for he stands all alone, and he waits for us continually, moaning and mourning until we come. And he hastens to bring us to him, for we are his joy and his delight, and he is the remedy of our life. . . . For love never allows him to be without pity; and when we fall into sin, and neglect recollection of him and the protection of our own soul, then Christ bears all alone the burden of us. And so he remains, moaning and mourning. Then it is for us in reverence and kindness to turn quickly to our Lord, and not to leave him alone.

⤳

BIBLICAL WISDOM

I am my beloved's,
and his desire is for me. Song of Songs 7:10

SILENCE FOR MEDITATION

QUESTIONS TO PONDER

- Julian makes a striking observation: when we are full of self-accusation, thinking this is holy, religious behavior, we end up neglecting the one at the center, Jesus himself. "Forget your flaws," Julian seems to say; "You're forgiven! Return in love to the one who loves you." How might Julian's observation challenge faith communities that stress human sin and God's wrath?
- What differences might you find between a faith community that believes God moans and mourns over us because of how sinful we are and one that

believes God moans and mourns over us because God is lonely for us, just as we are?

- What do you or your faith community believe about God desiring, longing, needing us?

PSALM FRAGMENT

I will listen to what the LORD God is saying;
for you speak peace to your faithful people
and to those who turn their hearts to you. Psalm 85:8 (ELW)

JOURNAL REFLECTIONS

- Waiting is part of the spiritual life; we spend Advent waiting and watching for our Lord's coming. Julian reminds us that Jesus waits for us as well—much more than we wait for him. What do you feel in response to Julian's words?
- Julian writes that Jesus "hastens to bring us to him, for we are his joy and his delight, and he is the remedy of our life." Do you feel that you are indeed his joy and delight? Why or why not?
- In what ways is Jesus the remedy of your life?

PRAYERS OF HOPE & HEALING

Pray for those afraid of being a burden to others; for those who have no one to care for them; for those who are caregivers for others.

PRAYER FOR TODAY

O God, desire of my heart, help me to trust and accept your even more powerful desire and love for me. Amen.

NOTES

Day 35

THE WISEST ACT IS FOR a creature to do according to the will and the counsels of [its] greatest and supreme friend. This blessed friend is Jesus, and it is his will and counsel that we keep with him and fasten ourselves closely to him, in whatever state we may be. For whether we be foul or clean, we are always the same in his love; for well or for woe, he wants us never to flee from him. . . . And so by knowledge and grace we may see our sin, profitably, without despair. . . . Also at that same time our courteous Lord revealed, most sweetly and most powerfully, the endlessness and the unchangeability of his love, and also his great goodness and his gracious protection of our spirit, so that the love between him and our souls will never be parted into eternity. And so in fear I have matter for meekness, which saves me from presumption, and in the blessed revelation of love I have matter for true comfort and for joy, which saves me from despair.

BIBLICAL WISDOM

I do not call you servants any longer, because the servant does not know what the master is doing; but I have called you friends, because I have made known to you everything that I have heard from my Father. John 15:15

SILENCE FOR MEDITATION

QUESTIONS TO PONDER

- Think of your favorite friends—presently or from the past. What characterizes a healthy friendship? How do these characteristics inform your relationship with Jesus, and his with you? How would you like to grow in his friendship?
- If Jesus' will and counsel is that we remain close to him, how might an individual's or faith community's closeness to him transform attitudes, feelings, and behaviors?

- Have you ever had a friendship of whole-hearted commitment? What contributes to (or gets in the way of) developing such closeness with friends—or with God?

PSALM FRAGMENT

One thing I ask of the LORD;,
one thing I seek;
that I may dwell in the house of the LORD
all the days of my life;
to gaze upon the beauty of the LORD
and to seek God in the temple. Psalm 27:4 (ELW)

JOURNAL REFLECTIONS

- Julian writes that Jesus wants us to "fasten ourselves closely to him." What does being close to Jesus mean to you? Does the thought of being close to Jesus attract you? Frighten you? Confuse or trouble you? Give you joy?
- Have you ever felt tempted to flee from Jesus? If so, why? And what happened? What helps you keep yourself "fastened closely to him"?
- Do you have a spiritual friend with whom you can share deeply about your faith life? If so, write about the relationship and what it means to you. If not, how might you go about finding a spiritual friend?

PRAYERS OF HOPE & HEALING

Pray for your friends, and for those who have no friends or mostly superficial bonds. Pray for all who are friends to the friendless, or who show kindness and care in unrecognized ways.

PRAYER FOR TODAY

Lord Jesus, friend of all, help me trust you and live as one whose life reveals your love and friendship to others. Amen.

NOTES

Journey

Day 36

AFTER ALL THESE REVELATIONS, THE *visions faded and Julian was returned to pain and dryness. When a priest visited, she told him she had been raving, seeming to discredit her own visions. She immediately regretted this and felt she had betrayed Jesus' exquisite mercy revealed to her. When she fell asleep she was visited by the devil in a terrible apparition; resisting the devil, she was returned to the consolation of her earlier visions.*

In response to her distress, feelings of betrayal, and torment by the devil: Our Lord very humbly revealed words to me, without voice and without opening of lips, just as he had done before, and said very sweetly: Know it well, it was no hallucination which you saw today, but accept and believe it and hold firmly to it, and comfort yourself with it and trust in it, and you will not be overcome. . . . And these words: You will not be overcome, were said very insistently and strongly, for certainty and strength against every tribulation which may come. He did not say, You will not be troubled, you will not be belabored, you will not be disquieted; but he said: You will not be overcome.

BIBLICAL WISDOM

We are afflicted in every way, but not crushed; perplexed, but not driven to despair; persecuted, but not forsaken; struck down, but not destroyed; always carrying in the body the death of Jesus, so that the life of Jesus may also be made visible in our bodies. 2 Corinthians 4:8-10

SILENCE FOR MEDITATION

QUESTIONS TO PONDER

- Even after all the beauty and grace of the visions God has given her, Julian slips again into doubt about their authenticity. Do you think she is denying her own worth when she tells the priest she had merely been raving ("Who, me? I'm not fit for 'real' visions.")? When you doubt the reality of God's love for you, is it God you are doubting or yourself? How do you know?

- Do you or your faith community believe such doubts come from the devil, as Julian did? Or from some unconscious part of ourselves? What purpose, if any, do such doubts serve?
- In response to Julian's distress, Jesus "did not say, You will not be troubled, you will not be belabored, you will not be disquieted; but he said: You will not be overcome." How do you respond to Jesus' promise to Julian? Do you find it consoling? Why or why not?

PSALM FRAGMENT

For the enemy has pursued me,
  crushing my life to the ground,
    making me sit in darkness like those long dead. . . .
Save me, O LORD, from my enemies;
  I have fled to you for refuge. Psalm 143:3, 9

JOURNAL REFLECTIONS

- To what temptations are you prone? What helps you resist temptation?
- Julian has come to know Jesus' voice through her visions. Where do you most clearly experience divine reality proclaimed, embodied, or offered to you?
- Jesus assures Julian (and you) that she will not be overcome despite whatever future tribulations may afflict her. If this is true, how might it shape the way you are in the world?

PRAYERS OF HOPE & HEALING

Pray for those who feel overwhelmed by social forces or their own circumstances, and for all who sing "we shall overcome" in the face of even the most apparently entrenched evil.

PRAYER FOR TODAY

Holy One, your promise overcomes all the forces that separate me from you and others. Help me hear you and trust you today. Amen.

NOTES

Day 37

ALL THIS FAMILIAR REVELATION OF our courteous Lord is a lesson of love. . . . For he wants us to know by the sweetness of his familiar love that all which we see or feel, within or without, which is in opposition to this is from the enemy and not from God. . . . If we are moved to be more careless about our way of life or about the custody of our heart, because we have knowledge of this plentiful love, then we have great need to beware of this impulse, should it come. It is false, and . . . has no resemblance to God's will. [Yet] when we have fallen through weakness or blindness, then our courteous Lord, touching us, moves us and protects us. . . . And with this our good Lord said most joyfully: See how I love you, as if he had said, my darling, behold and see your Lord, your God, who is your Creator and your endless joy; see your own brother, your savior; my child, behold and see what delight and bliss I have in your salvation.

BIBLICAL WISDOM

You shall be called by a new name
that the mouth of the LORD will give.
You shall be a crown of beauty in the hand of the LORD,
and a royal diadem in the hand of your God. Isaiah 62:2b-3

SILENCE FOR MEDITATION

QUESTIONS TO PONDER

- Julian teaches that anything that opposes our abiding in Jesus' love is "from the enemy and not from God." Does this ring true to your experience? How?
- How might a faith community help its members discern what is of God and what is not?

- Julian reminds us also, however, that the unconditional nature of God's love doesn't give us permission to be "careless about our way of life or . . . the custody of our heart." What is the relationship between God's pure grace and the lifestyles we follow, or the things, ideas, and people to whom we give our hearts? If all is forgiven, does that mean "anything goes"?

PSALM FRAGMENT

Teach me to do your will,
for you are my God.
Let your good spirit lead me
on a level path. Psalm 143:10

JOURNAL REFLECTIONS

- Jesus says to Julian (and you), "See how I love you!" Reflect in your journal about how careful you are of this love in your daily life. To what or to whom do you give custody of your heart?
- According to Julian, Jesus is "your Lord, your God . . . your Creator . . . your endless joy . . . your own brother, your savior." Which of these images speaks most dearly to you? Why? If you have some other favorite name or image of Jesus, write about it. Try using a new name for Jesus in your prayer.
- Julian wrote a book to pass on the astonishing love of God she had received. How does your life pass on the astonishing love of God?

PRAYERS OF HOPE & HEALING

Pray for those who struggle to discern God's call and leading, and for those who are constrained by poverty or other limits from living the fullness of God's abundant love for them.

PRAYER FOR TODAY

O Lord, give me ears to discern your voice in all the places you are inviting me deeper into your love. Amen.

NOTES

GOD REVEALED ALL THIS MOST blessedly, as though to say: See, I am God. See, I am in all things. See, I do all things. See, I never remove my hands from my works, nor ever shall without end. See, I guide all things to the end that I ordain them for, before time began, with the same power and wisdom and love with which I made them: how should anything be amiss? . . . In this endless love we are led and protected by God, and we shall never be lost. . . . And just as we were to be without end, so we were treasured and hidden in God, known and loved from without beginning. I saw . . . in everything that before God made us he loved us, which love was never abated and never will be. And in this love he has done all his works . . . and in this love our life is everlasting. In our creation we had beginning, but the love in which he created us was in him from without beginning. In this love we have our beginning, and all this shall we see in God without end.

⌐

BIBLICAL WISDOM

Shower, O heavens, from above,
*   and let the skies rain down righteousness;*
let the earth open, that salvation may spring up,
*   and let it cause righteousness to sprout up also;*
I the LORD have created it. Isaiah 45:8

SILENCE FOR MEDITATION

QUESTIONS TO PONDER

- Julian asserts that God sustains all things. How do you see this sustaining action of God at work in all things? What kinds of questions (scientific, moral, existential) make faith in God's sustenance of the cosmos difficult for you? How does your faith community handle these questions?

- Where, if at all, in your own life, a loved one's life, your community, or our world do you struggle to see God's loving hand guiding the situation?
- Why, if God has loved each of us and all things endlessly from before the world's beginning, is there so much pain in the world? Why do we resist living in God's love?

PSALM FRAGMENT

Mark this –
  God is our God forever and ever,
  guiding us even to the end. Psalm 48:14 (ELW)

JOURNAL REFLECTIONS

- Julian writes that God guides all things to the end ordained for them. Is this a comfort for you? Why or why not? To what end do you think God has ordained you?
- Julian portrays a God profoundly engaged in the creation and guiding of reality: thus, "how should anything be amiss?" Talk to God about what, in your view, *is* amiss in the world (or your world). Journal about this dialogue.
- Julian insists that God is in all things. That would include you and all those you struggle to love. Write about a particular person (yourself or someone else) glimpsed through such love.

PRAYERS OF HOPE & HEALING

Pray for the natural world, created by God with exquisite care and love. Pray for each human being, perfectly fashioned by God.

PRAYER FOR TODAY

Lord God, help me trust that you created me in love just as I am. Give me eyes to see your beauty in every person, in every creature and plant, cloud and lake and star. Amen.

NOTES

Day 39

FROM THE TIME [THESE SHOWINGS were] revealed, I desired many times to know in what was our Lord's meaning. And fifteen years after and more, I was answered in spiritual understanding, and it was said: What, do you wish to know your Lord's meaning in this thing? Know it well, love was his meaning. Who reveals it to you? Love. What did he reveal to you? Love. Why does he reveal it to you? For love. Remain in this, and you will know more of the same. But you will never know different, without end.

˜

BIBLICAL WISDOM

As the Father has loved me, so I have loved you; abide in my love. John 15:9

SILENCE FOR MEDITATION

QUESTIONS TO PONDER

- Love is the beginning and the end of all Julian's visions—indeed (as she sees it), of all reality itself. In what ways do our culture's values conflict with Julian's understanding?
- Abiding in love can sound easy; but consider the agony of truly facing ourselves and letting God's love probe deep, shadowy, or shameful aspects of our hearts—or consider letting this love free us from destructive patterns or addictions into new life. How does God's probing, relentless, liberating love differ from cheap grace (grace that makes no claim upon us)?
- "Remain in this [love], and you will know more of the same. But you will never know different, without end." How has your experience of God's love changed over the years?

Psalm Fragment

How precious is your steadfast love, O God!
All people may take refuge in the shadow of your wings.
They feast on the abundance of your house,
and you give them drink from the river of your delights.
For with you is the fountain of life;
in your light we see light. Psalm 36:7-9

Journal Reflections

- Psalm 36:7-9 gives many images of God's love: "refuge in the shadow of your wings," "river of your delights," "fountain of life," the light by which we see all light, and so on. In your journal, use these images to frame questions, reflections, or prayer on God's love for you.
- It took fifteen years of prayer about these visions for Julian to discern their core meaning in Christ: "Love was his meaning." Write of an experience whose deep meaning was revealed only years later—or one whose meaning you are still discerning in prayer.
- An ancient Christian name for God is "Lover of souls." Pray to God using this name today: "Lover of my soul . . ." What feelings does this name evoke in you? What sort of life or vocation might flow from a relationship with such a God?

Prayers of Hope & Healing

Pray for those enmeshed in situations of war, trauma, homelessness, or addiction, for whom the love of God seems absent from their daily reality. Pray for those who seek to reveal love even there.

Prayer for Today

Lover of my soul, open your love, saturating all things that I may truly and fully abide in you this day. Amen.

Notes

Day 40

ALL WILL BE WELL, AND all will be well, and all manner of thing will be well. . . . [For] I may make all things well, and I can make all things well, and I shall make all things well, and I will make all things well. . . . And [in the bliss of heaven] it will truly be made known to us what he means in the sweet words when he says: All will be well, and you will see it yourself, that every kind of thing will be well. And then will the bliss of our motherhood in Christ be to begin anew in the joys of our Father, God, which new beginning will last, newly beginning without end. . . . God wants us . . . always to be strong in faithful trust, in well-being and in woe, for he loves us and delights in us, and so he wishes us to love him and delight in him and trust greatly in him, and all will be well.

❧

BIBLICAL WISDOM

And the one who was seated on the throne said, "See, I am making all things new." Also he said, "Write this, for these words are trustworthy and true." Then he said to me, "It is done! I am the Alpha and the Omega, the beginning and the end. To the thirsty I will give water as a gift from the spring of the water of life. Revelation 21:5-6

SILENCE FOR MEDITATION

QUESTIONS TO PONDER

- Julian's visions, like the Bible itself, culminate in the eschaton: the end of time and the fullness of heaven and earth, when God will be all in all. Write about your own image of heaven.
- Centered endlessly in love, Julian's experience of God moves toward hope. What difference does the vision of an utterly certain hope grounding our universe make in how we live our lives in Christ?

- What in our culture argues against Julian's faith that "all will be well"? Is Christian faith both counterintuitive and countercultural? Why or why not? What are the implications for both individual Christians and communities of faith in living this hope?

PSALM FRAGMENT

You have turned my mourning into dancing;
*   you have taken off my sackcloth*
*   and clothed me with joy,*
so that my soul may praise you and not be silent.
*   O LORD my God, I will give thanks to you forever.* Psalm 30:11-12

JOURNAL REFLECTIONS

- "You will see it yourself, that every kind of thing will be well." Write your vision of how a restored creation, or your own life's hopes, would look unfolded in God's ultimate reality. Express these hopes to God.
- As you ponder God's promise that all will be well, ask God whatever questions arise about the meaning or use of your own life. How might God be wanting you to participate in the wellness of all creation?
- "All will be well, and all will be well, and all manner of thing will be well"—for you and for all things. Let these grace-full words echo in you as you go forth from these forty days to love as God invites you. May you know the truth of God's endless love for you!

PRAYERS OF HOPE & HEALING

Pray for those who despair that all will be well for them and their world. Pray for children, artists of all kinds, and visionaries like Julian who help us live in the hope God intends for all things.

PRAYER FOR TODAY

Holy God, lover of all things, let your strong hope fill my life, my vocation, and my love of you. Thank you for your love that will make all things well. Amen.

NOTES

JOURNEY'S END

You have finished your *40-Day Journey with Julian of Norwich*. I hope it has been a good journey and that along the way you have learned much, experienced much, and found good resources to deepen your faith and practice. As a result of this journey:

- How are you different?
- What have you learned?
- What have you experienced?
- In what ways have your faith and practice been transformed?

NOTES

FOR FURTHER READING

MIDDLE-ENGLISH PRIMARY EDITIONS

Julian of Norwich. *A Book of Showings to the Anchoress Julian of Norwich.* Ed. Edmund Colledge, O.S.A., and James Walsh, S.J. Toronto: Pontifical Institute of Medieval Studies, 1978.

————. *The Shewings of Julian of Norwich.* Ed. Georgia Ronan Crampton. TEAMS Middle English Texts Series. Kalamazoo, Mich.: Medieval Institute Publications/Western Michigan University, 1994.

————. *The Writings of Julian of Norwich:* A Vision Showed to a Devout Woman *and* A Revelation of Love. Ed. Nicholas Watson and Jacqueline Jenkins. University Park, Pa.: Pennsylvania State University Press, 2006.

MODERN ENGLISH VERSIONS

Julian of Norwich. *A Lesson of Love: The Revelations of Julian of Norwich.* Trans. and ed. Fr. John-Julian, O.J.N. New York: Walker and Company, 1988.

————. *Showings.* Trans. and ed. Edmund Colledge, O.S.A., and James Walsh, S.J. Classics of Western Spirituality Series. Mahwah, N.J.: Paulist Press, 1978.

BOOKS ABOUT JULIAN OF NORWICH

Durka, Gloria. *Praying with Julian of Norwich.* Companions for the Journey Series. Winona, Minn.: St. Mary's Press, 1989.

Hide, Kerrie. *Gifted Origins to Graced Fulfillment: The Soteriology of Julian of Norwich.* Collegeville, Minn.: Liturgical Press, 2001.

Jantzen, Grace M. *Julian of Norwich: Mystic and Theologian*. Mahwah, N.J.: Paulist Press, 1987.

Nuth, Joan M. *Wisdom's Daughter: The Theology of Julian of Norwich*. New York: Crossroad, 1991.

Obbard, Elizabeth Ruth. *Through Julian's Windows: Growing into Wholeness with Julian of Norwich*. Norwich: The Canterbury Press, 2008.

————. *See How I Love You: Meditating on the Way of the Cross with Julian of Norwich*. Norwich: The Canterbury Press, 1996.

Upjohn, Sheila. *Why Julian Now? A Voyage of Discovery*. Grand Rapids, Mich.: Eerdmans, 1997.

SOURCES

All readings are taken from *Showings* by Julian of Norwich, translated from the critical text with an introduction by Edmund Colledge, O.S.A., and James Walsh, S.J., Classics of Western Spirituality Series (Mahwah, N.J.: Paulist Press), 1978. Note that Julian's writing does not use gender-inclusive language with regard to God. Most of Julian's God-references pertain to Jesus (as in the quote opening the Preface, in which Jesus is named "Love"), so the masculine pronouns are not inappropriate. But there are cases where she refers to the Triune God or to the First or Third Person of the Trinity using masculine language as well.

Day 1: 186, 194.

Day 2: 181, 213.

Day 3: 130f.

Day 4: 131, 132.

Day 5: 131.

Day 6: 204, 205, 280.

Day 7: 198, 240, 328.

Day 8: 207, 230f., 326.

Day 9: 211f.

Day 10: 201f.

Day 11: 216, 217.

Day 12: 225, 226.

Day 13: 227f., 229, 232.

Day 14: 231, 246.

Day 15: 245, 247, 154.

Day 16: 248f., 251.

Day 17: 248, 249, 252, 254.

Day 18: 254, 255.

Day 19: 201, 259, 262.

Day 20: 266.

Day 21: 267, 270.

Day 22: 274f., 276, 271.

Day 23: 282, 283.

Day 24: 312f., 164, 285, 337.

Day 25: 313, 289.

Day 26: 241, 264, 265.

Day 27: 293, 294, 295.

Day 28: 295, 297, 298, 304.

Day 29: 298f

Day 30: 301, 302.

Day 31: 329, 330.

Day 32: 300, 281.

Day 33: 325.

Day 34: 334f., 336.

Day 35: 329, 332, 334.

Day 36: (explanatory material in italics, 310–12), 314, 315.

Day 37: 334, 221.

Day 38: 199, 284, 342f

Day 39: 342.

Day 40: 225, 229, 305, 315.

NOTES

1   Julian of Norwich, *Showings,* ed. E. Colledge and J. Walsh, Classics of Western Spirituality Series (Mahwah, N.J.: Paulist Press, 1978), 342. See note on page 107 regarding gendered God-language in Julian's writings.

2   Rowan Williams, Archbishop of Canterbury, as quoted on the back cover of Nicholas Watson and Jacqueline Jenkins, eds., *The Writings of Julian of Norwich* (University Park, Pa.: Pennsylvania State University Press, 2006).

3   Julian of Norwich, 343.

4   Evelyn Underhill's widely read study, *Mysticism,* was an initial introduction of Julian on a wider scale. Julian was also cited in important poems and novels of the twentieth century (including T. S. Eliot's "Little Gidding," Iris Murdoch's *Nuns and Soldiers,* and Denise Levertov's cycle of poems, "The Showings: Lady Julian of Norwich 1342–1416"). For an overview of contemporary literary and theological reception of Julian, see "Mysticism and Spirituality: 1670–2000" in the introduction to Nicholas Watson and Jacqueline Jenkins, eds., *The Writings of Julian of Norwich* (University Park, Pa.: Pennsylvania State University Press, 2006), 17–24. The 1978 two-volume critical edition and commentary by Edmund Colledge and James Walsh provided a breakthrough for broader readership and also formed the basis of the Classics of Western Spirituality volume (published by Paulist Press) used in the present book.

NOTES

NOTES

NOTES